lessons in
SERVICE

from
CHARLIE
TROTTER

lessons in
SERVICE
from
CHARLIE
TROTTER

Edmund Lawler

TEN SPEED PRESS
Berkeley ■ Toronto

FOR PRISCILLA, MY SWEETHEART

Ten Speed Press
Box 7123
Berkeley, California 94707
www.tenspeed.com

Distributed in Australia by Simon & Schuster Australia, in Canada by Ten Speed Press
Canada, in New Zealand by Southern Publishers Group, in South Africa by Real Books,
in Southeast Asia by Berkeley Books, and in the United Kingdom and Europe by Airlift
Book Company.

Cover and text design by Toni Tajima
Cover and page ii photos by Michael Voltattorni

Library of Congress Cataloging-in-Publication Data
Lawler, Ed.
  Lessons in service from Charlie Trotter / Edmund Lawler.
    p. cm.
Includes index.
  ISBN 1-58008-315-3
  1. Restaurant management. 2. Charlie Trotter's (Restaurant) I.
Trotter, Charlie. II. Title.
  TX911.3.M27 L417 2001
  647.95'068--dc21

                            2001004439

Printed in Canada
First printing, 2001

1 2 3 4 5 6 7 8 9 10 — 05 04 03 02 01

CONTENTS

ACKNOWLEDGMENTS   vi

INTRODUCTION: Magical Mystery Tour —
An Evening at Charlie Trotter's   1

PART I: Knowing Your Business and Your Customer
1. Charlie Trotter and His Weird Sense of Attention to Detail   13
2. Reading the Customer's Mind   27

PART II: Leading: Hiring, Motivating, and Training Your Staff
3. Help Wanted: A Passion for Service   43
4. Stoking the Fires of Passion   61
5. Learning the Ropes on a Tight Ship   83

PART III: Executing:
Making Great Service Happen Every Day
6. Building a One-on-One Customer Relationship   105
7. Back Stage at Charlie Trotter's   121
8. On Murphy's Law and the Rules of Recovery   143

PART IV: Exceeding Expectations:
Attracting Lifelong Customers
9. Going the Extra Mile (or Four) for the Customer   163
10. Travels with Charlie   185
11. Goodwill Hunting   201

CONCLUSION: It's the Journey, Not the Destination   221

INDEX   227

ACKNOWLEDGMENTS

My thanks to Charlie Trotter for making his staff, his restaurant, and himself available during the reporting and writing phases of this book. As he did when I wrote a previous book about his restaurant, Charlie gave me the run of the house.

Both announced and unannounced, I dropped in on training sessions, preservice meetings, and special events. Many nights, I simply observed—from the controlled fury of the kitchen to the calm of the tree-lined curb where the valets greet the guests. The front-of-the house staff were ever gracious and always cooperative, even on days when their preservice tasks were piling up as they spent time with me.

Three staff members at the restaurant were particularly helpful—Mark Signorio, Paul Larson, and Mary Hegeman. Mark's guidance and his institutional memory of the restaurant were invaluable. Paul Larson helped arrange interviews, alerted me to training sessions, and rode herd on the personal essays on service the staff wrote for me. Mary tracked down names, numbers, and countless other details. She also helped me track down Chef Trotter for interviews and more impromptu sessions with him when I needed to tie up loose ends from a previous interview.

I am in debt to Julie Bennett, my editor at Ten Speed Press. Her keen vision allowed her to see things both large and small in the manuscript. Finally, I want to thank my family, who patiently endured my absences in the weeks leading up to the deadline.

INTRODUCTION

A Magical Mystery Tour

I t's a magical space of tranquility and elegance just steps from the bustle of a congested big-city neighborhood. Within this sanctuary guests are served some of the most brilliantly conceived food in the world—tiny jewels on delicate white china—deftly matched with wines from three redwood cellars.

Orchestrating the interplay of food and wine is a team of dark-suited servers who move gracefully through the dining room, all but anticipating the guests' every need. Gracious to a fault, the impeccably groomed servers never say no to a guest's request. Their mission is to guide a guest through the dining experience of a lifetime—to "blow their minds."

A visit to what many believe is the best restaurant in America begins with a phone call during which a reservationist at Charlie Trotter's provides a brief overview of the dining experience. "We serve a multicourse tasting menu. Expect to spend about three hours with us," a guest is told. "We're a nonsmoking restaurant, and gentlemen are expected to wear jackets." This primer hardly does the restaurant justice, but the phones are ringing, and ringing. The

1

restaurant is booked on weekends for three months in advance. Securing the restaurant's most coveted prize—the kitchen table— requires a reservation six months out.

FOLLOW THE RED-BRICK ROAD

When the evening finally arrives, a valet greets guests at the curb, stepping forward to meet incoming cars, cabs, and limos. After assisting them from their vehicle, he escorts the guests along a short path of red inlaid bricks and up several steps to the restaurant's front door. Posted discreetly outside the door is a brass plaque designating Charlie Trotter's as a member of Relais & Chateaux, a registry of the world's top hotels and restaurants.

A receptionist warmly greets the guests at the front door and invites them into the foyer of the two-story, almost century-old brownstone. The foyer is a visually stunning atrium whose vertical features are accented with a nearly floor-to-ceiling wine rack and, on the opposite wall, a lithograph by German painter Joseph Müller titled "Two Bathing Ladies." But artwork is kept to a minimum throughout the restaurant. The artistry is on the plate.

If there is a short delay until the guests' table is ready, Trotter's congenial front-of-the house staff will take the guests' coats and bags and offer a welcoming glass of champagne, or if they prefer, a glass of wine. For guests who've dined at Trotter's before—and they are legion—the brief stop allows time to renew acquaintances with the staff. "Oh, it's so nice to see you again," is a commonly heard greeting. Returning guests, or friends of the restaurant as they are known, appreciate the gesture of recognition. They feel like they're home, in the company of good friends and the comfort of good food.

WELCOME TO THE PROMISED LAND

First-time diners are told about the grand time that awaits them. Some guests require a bit of reassurance once they've stepped into the culinary temple of five-diamond and five-star dining. Charlie Trotter's won the 2000 Outstanding Restaurant Award from the James Beard Foundation—the most prestigious award in the American food world—and was named America's Best Restaurant that same year by *Wine Spectator*. Accolades adorn the walls in the restaurant's second-story corporate office.

If the knees of the uninitiated are knocking in anticipation of such an awesome event, the staff will instantly sense their discomfort and put them at ease. A receptionist or a manager will whet their appetites with descriptions of the restaurant's two degustation menus and the voluminous wine list representing all the leading wine-producing regions of the world. "You're going to have a great time." And the service staff will see to it that they do.

From the foyer-atrium, guests are led either into a first-floor dining room or to one of two dining rooms on the second floor. Each one is intimate, about thirty seats in a room. The dining rooms are gently lit and subtly appointed with mahogany wainscoting, custom-woven wall fabric, silk draperies, and simple wall sconces. In sharp contrast to the austerity of the rooms are riotously colorful floral displays situated on marble-topped serving credenzas in the heart of each room.

NO DETAIL IS TOO SMALL

The tables have been meticulously prepared. Exquisite flatware, Wedgewood china bearing a distinctive T, and Riedel stemware so delicate that annual breakage costs exceed $40,000 are set against the canvas of crisp, white linen tablecloths.

Once the guests are seated, a server gives them a brief introduction to how the evening will unfold. Menus are presented. A

$115 grand menu might feature a parade of such dishes as marinated hamachi with osetra caviar, pomelo, and pulped avocado; seared Maine diver scallops with Kumamoto oyster sauce and braised kohlrabi; and ragout of squab, rabbit saddle, and lamb tongue with caramelized cauliflower and black truffle emulsion.

A $100 vegetable menu would be no less grand. It might feature chestnut soup with vaucluse black truffles and brussels sprouts, ragout of roasted organic root vegetables served with braised legumes, and butternut squash pithivier with coriander caramel.

IT'S YOUR CALL

Servers are quick to point out that if the menus are not to the guests' liking, the kitchen will be happy to customize a course of dishes more to their tastes. Flexibility is the rule of the house, and guests drive the dining experience if they wish. However, guests may simply entrust their evening to the kitchen, which is more than happy to customize a series of dishes that are designed around either wine preferences or individual culinary tastes.

A sommelier will visit the table and help diners navigate an adventurous, fifty-five-page wine list of more than 1,500 selections with special emphasis on Burgundy, the Rhine, and wineries from California to Australia. Guests can pay from $30 up to $14,000 per bottle.

A steady stream of dishes will begin to arrive, yet the pace in the room of smartly dressed diners remains relaxed and unhurried. Oohs and ahhs over an arriving dish punctuate quiet conversations. Neat, well-spoken servers explain the provenance of each dish. Rather than hover at a table, they step back into the "weeds"—the room's periphery—where they study each of their tables, anticipating guests' needs and the arrival of more courses.

Servers at Trotter's are renowned for their willingness to provide the little extras that their counterparts at other restaurants would never dream of offering. But unlike at other restaurants, servers at Trotter's are empowered to interpret each table's needs. An extra course of food, an extra bottle of wine, a reduction in the bill to compensate for a flaw, or perhaps a free cookbook or a logoed Trotter's baseball cap—they're all part of the value-added service that a server brings to a table. And the servers make those decisions without any second-guessing by the management.

IGNORE THE MAN BEHIND THE CURTAIN

Although service is precise, it's not robotic. The four-to-five-member service teams in each of the restaurant's three dining rooms establish a ballet-like rhythm that's "flawless, spontaneous, and beautiful," in the words of chef-owner Charlie Trotter, the culinary wizard who remains largely hidden behind the curtain in his state-of-the-art kitchen.

As he obsesses over each dish that passes under his discerning eye en route to a guest's table, Trotter methodically gathers intelligence about diners' reactions from his front-of-the-house staff. "Table 44 is psyched. They love the salmon," reports a server, which is music to Trotter's ears. Now psyched himself, he will exhort his team of world-class chefs to take whatever culinary steps are necessary to push the guest over the edge from the ordinary to the extraordinary. Unlike the dining rooms, the pace in the kitchen is feverish as twenty chefs craft the night's grand cuisine with the focused intensity of a surgeon and his team at an operating table. And Trotter is always willing to turn up the heat.

Beyond the kitchen's doors, the three-hour dining experience begins to wind down for the guests—but not without a grand finale. Dessert, often a flight of desserts, will put an exclamation point on the evening and leave a lasting impression. Guests are often handed souvenirs at the end of the evening. Trotter may have signed their menus, the label from the bottle of wine they so enjoyed may be presented to them, or they might be given hand-made mignardises—tiny candies—in wooden boxes so beautiful that they look like collector's items. Guests are also given a customer satisfaction survey that allows them to evaluate the service, the food, the wine, and the bottom line: "Did you enjoy your evening?"

INSIDE LOOKING OUT

Perhaps they'd like to see the kitchen, the wine cellars, or the studio kitchen where Trotter tapes his Public Broadcasting System series *The Kitchen Sessions with Charlie Trotter*. No part of the restaurant is off-limits to the guests. In the kitchen, which underwent a $750,000 renovation several years ago, guests can marvel at the cleanliness of the room where ceiling-mounted smoke eaters purify the air and remove airborne grime. The kitchen's focal point is a huge French-made cooking suite with three gas-fired ovens, two large flat-tops, and four radiant heating units. Trotter will usually come up for air long enough to say hello to guests.

With guests in tow, the server will proceed downstairs to the softly lit, temperature- and humidity-controlled redwood cellars that house the bulk of the restaurant's $1 million, 25,000-bottle wine collection. Guests are like kids in a candy store as they sweep past row after row of rare vintages. Servers enliven the tour with tales of a wine's heroic passage—like the one that was recovered from a ship that had sunk to the floor of the Baltic Sea after being torpedoed in World War I by a German U-boat.

Back upstairs, guests are brought to the studio kitchen. Except for a ceiling-mounted camera and a pair of large TV monitors, the room doesn't look much like a Hollywood sound stage. In fact, on most nights, private parties are held in the studio kitchen's twenty-seat dining room.

Finally guests are escorted to the foyer-atrium where they are bid farewell. Trotter will sometimes appear there at the end of the second seating in the wee hours of the morning to chat with guests, sign menus or one his cookbooks, or pose for pictures.

Rather than tidy up their stations and head for home after a night of intense mental and physical concentration, service staff members will also appear in the atrium-foyer at the close of the second seating to lend guests a hand. They'll escort them to the curb and help the valet flag down a cab. And they'll always tell the guests how sincerely they'd like to see them return. And who wouldn't want to take them up on their kind offer?

AN EXEMPLAR OF SERVICE

That completes the chef's tour. Now let's tour Charlie Trotter's *Lessons in Service*. The book is divided into four main sections. Part I, "Knowing Your Business and Your Customer," serves up advice on how to anticipate customer needs rather than simply react to them. Great service providers like those at Charlie Trotter's have an almost sixth sense for what guests would like. But more than that, Charlie Trotter truly believes that no business can succeed until it identifies exactly how its customer service reps treat its customers or clients. In Trotter's case, customers are given the white-glove treatment. The service team treat customers in the same gracious way that they would like to be treated themselves. It's Charlie's Golden Rule.

Part II, "Leading: Hiring, Motivating, and Training Your Staff," offers invaluable advice on hiring, motivating, and training a service staff. You'll discover that Trotter's techniques in these critical areas are unorthodox, but they work. Service providers have a whole menu of innovative ideas to choose from in this section.

Part III, "Executing: Making Great Service Happen Every Day," explains how Charlie Trotter's consistently exceeds customer expectations. Ever the perfectionist, Trotter allows that no evening at his restaurant has ever been flawless, but his staff has a knack for performing at a level of excellence that few businesses match. One secret to success: Trotter actively and methodically listens to his customers' complaints, compliments, and suggestions.

The final section of the book, Part IV, "Exceeding Expectations: Attracting Lifelong Customers," looks at how Trotter's engenders a sense of loyalty among customers by establishing relationships with them. The relationship building extends to the neighborhood, the culinary community, and the philanthropic community. This section also looks at how Trotter's service philosophy plays out not only in the restaurant but in out-of-house events and its non-restaurant ventures, such as its new retail outlet, Trotter's To Go.

Throughout the book you will hear the voices of the restaurant's customers, its service staff, and its food purveyors as they explain in their own words what makes the restaurant unique.

Charlie Trotter would never attempt to tell another business how to operate. The restaurant business is the only one he knows. But he does welcomes other service providers—hospitals, hotels, airlines, financial institutions, schools, consulting firms, cab companies, telecommunications companies, and of course restaurants— to borrow liberally from his playbook on how to treat a customer.

Each chapter in the book concludes with a series of Service Points. Designed to be universal in nature, they are easily applicable to just about any service-based business—including yours. Businesses that assiduously apply these lessons in service can create a magical mix of more careful attention to detail, both large and small; a more empathetic sense for the customer; and a passion for delivering the best possible product or service.

PART I

KNOWING YOUR

BUSINESS AND

YOUR CUSTOMER

Competence and fairness are merely the price of admission when it comes to customer service at Charlie Trotter's. Learn how Charlie Trotter's takes customer service to a higher plane by being sensitive, almost clairvoyant, about customer needs in a restaurant where no task is more or less significant than the next.

1

Charlie Trotter and His Weird Sense of Attention to Detail

I f your business can't get the little things right, what are the chances of mastering the larger matters? At Charlie Trotter's, where an evening is essentially an accumulation of little things done right, the intensely customer-focused service staff sweats the small stuff. Such attention to detail costs a business nothing.

Charlie Trotter's service philosophy springs from the simple question: "How would I like to be treated if I were the guest?" Like royalty, of course, although Trotter forgoes the regal trappings in favor of sincere, gracious, and flawless service.

Trotter himself would resist being treated like a king. "I would rather provide service than be served," he says. "I have a hard time when people are waiting on me. Too many people mistake serving for servitude where you subordinate yourself socially or economically to the person you are serving."

He believes there's a true nobility to service. His twenty-two-person front-of-the-house team (which includes servers, sommeliers, food runners, dining room managers, and receptionists) executes his personal vision of sincere, dignified service on a nightly basis in the intimacy of a nearly hundred-year-old, two-story townhouse in Chicago's Lincoln Park neighborhood.

Diners who feast on his brilliantly conceived dishes are to be treated with the same degree of care and respect they would receive in Trotter's own home. Trotter has scrupulously schooled his staff to never say no to a diner's request, even when it seems to border on the ridiculous. Well-dressed, well-spoken, and well-versed in the products they serve, the Trotter team have elevated service to an almost operatic status.

In an age when service workers sometimes seem to resent interaction with a customer, Trotter's service team is devoid of such antagonism. Trotter has no tolerance for employees who would dare to bite the hand that feeds them. The service team have a deep appreciation of their guests. For without them, there would be no Charlie Trotter's.

ENJOYING HIS JUST DESSERTS

On the night he accepted the Outstanding Chef Award at the 1999 James Beard Foundation Awards, Trotter declared that service is as important as or more important than the food, and that that is the first thing a chef has to understand. Although he was hardly ungrateful for the award for which he'd been a finalist for five years previous, Trotter admitted that he would have traded the Outstanding Chef Award for the Outstanding Restaurant Award. "That's more important to me." Trotter received his just desserts only a year later when the Beard Foundation honored his restaurant with the Outstanding Restaurant Award, the equivalent of an Oscar for the year's best picture.

No detail is too insignificant for the much-decorated Trotter and his service team, and no single element is more important than the next. In other words, the restrooms are tended with the same degree of care as the presentation of the restaurant's $115-per-plate grand menu. In the kitchen, Trotter's chefs are fond of saying that it's just as important to carefully close a glass door on a cabinet as it is to sauté a chicken. Let one small detail slip and the larger, seemingly more important matters begin to suffer as well. But that would never happen at Charlie Trotter's.

"Charlie Trotter's is a highly tuned machine. There's an organizational brilliance to the service."

Ray Harris, Wall Street financier who has eaten at Charlie Trotter's nearly 300 times

Newsweek asked its readers in a July 31, 2000, article headlined "Management à la Trotter" what it would be like if Trotter applied his golden rule of service to driving a cab. The article said, "If Charlie Trotter, the famously perfectionist Chicago chef drove a cab, its door handles would gleam like polished flatware, and if you weren't satisfied with your ride, he'd offer to drive you somewhere else, gratis.

"It would be so easy to say, 'Hi, how're you doing?' he mused recently, apropos of his favorite topic: why the rest of the world can't be more like Charlie Trotter's restaurant. 'Where can I take you today? Do you have a preferred route?' So of course you'd want Charlie Trotter as your cab driver even if, based on the prices in his restaurant, a ride to Chicago from O'Hare might set you back $175 before tax and tip."

LET THE CUSTOMER BE DAMNED

Trotter wishes that more people in the service industry would simply think about all the things they could do to go the extra mile on behalf of a customer. But the extra mile—much less the extra step—may be too much to ask. "To me it's just doing the obvious. It's just common sense." He recalled watching postal workers in his neighborhood routinely leave the gates open after they've delivered the mail. It would be so simple to pull the gate shut. Or it would be so simple for a retail clerk to wrest himself from a long-running personal phone call and come to the rescue of a customer who appears lost or confused. Or it would be so simple for a florist to call a customer to inform her that the delivery of her flowers has been delayed. Or perhaps you've heard the story about a customer in a well-known seafood chain restaurant who complained to her server that the food was too cold. The server stuck his finger in the food and declared its temperature just right.

The oldest of four children, Charlie Trotter was born with an instinct for getting the little things right, although he chafes at the notion that he's a perfectionist. "Let's just say I'm an 'excellentist' because perfection is an unattainable goal. Perfection isn't that interesting. It is more interesting to do things with sincerity and a certain quirkiness. With perfection there's no tolerance for failure, and there are enormous benefits to failure because of the valuable lessons they impart."

Call it perfection or call it excellence, Trotter has always pursued it with a relentless—some would say fanatic—zeal. Unfortunately for most service providers, even mediocrity seems like an unattainable goal.

Ironically, Trotter, who majored in political science at the University of Wisconsin, found himself being

"Charlie Trotter is demanding and tough, but he helps educate us. The more he tells about what he needs, the better we can meet his objectives, because the farm is where it all starts. Every detail is important to him. We consider ourselves a part of his team—an extension of his kitchen. We will do everything to fight and scrape to remain a part of his team. There is nothing we wouldn't do for him."

Lee Jones, marketing director of The Chef's Garden in Huron, Ohio, a family farm that produces culinary delicacies for Charlie Trotter's and other top restaurants

drawn to the restaurant business, where perfection is more the exception than the rule. In Madison, he tended bar, waited tables, and began cooking for his friends, who seemed to appreciate his early, and occasionally overcooked, forays into the culinary arts.

BITTEN BY THE RESTAURANT BUG

Discovering that he had a flair for cooking, Trotter began charting a career in the restaurant business. He was impressed with the energy level and the dynamic, electric atmosphere of some restaurants. He was also struck by how much better restaurants could run their businesses—from the kitchen to the bar to the dining room. There seemed to be an industry-wide tolerance for things that weren't quite right—broken doors, half-baked food, and service that was indifferent at best. "Here, we have an almost weird sense of attention to detail," he says.

After graduating from Wisconsin and returning home to Wilmette, a North Shore suburb of Chicago, Trotter began his career on the ground floor by waiting tables for one of the best-run restaurants in the country—Sinclairs, owned by Gordon Sinclair. Famed chef Norman Van Aken allowed Trotter to learn the craft at his restaurant, first in the dining room as a waiter and later in the kitchen as a line chef.

Trotter knew he had found a home and then explained to his father, Bob, that cooking was not some passing fancy. He wanted to open his own restaurant. Although his father, the owner of an executive recruiting firm and himself the possessor of a keen eye for detail, had serious reservations about restaurants as viable businesses, he agreed to help financially support his son's dream of owning and operating a restaurant.

GO WEST YOUNG CHEF

But Charlie Trotter realized he was a long way from being ready to launch a restaurant, especially in a market as competitive as Chicago's. He headed west to attend the California Culinary Academy in San Francisco to be formally schooled in the culinary arts. Restless and eager to get back in the kitchen, he dropped out of school after only four months. He remained in San Francisco, where he cooked at several restaurants and the Hotel Meridien. Not far away was the Napa Valley, which Trotter visited frequently to develop a deeper appreciation of wine.

From San Francisco, Trotter moved to Florida, where he rejoined his mentor Norman Van Aken and restauranteur Gordon Sinclair at a new restaurant called Sinclair's North American Grill. Trotter occasionally visited New York, where he dined in some of that city's most renowned restaurants. He expected to be overwhelmed by the experience, but wasn't. What he was impressed with, however, was how some of the top gourmet restaurants operated from stately brownstones in the city rather than from the ground or top floors of office buildings or hotels. He found the brownstone atmosphere more welcoming and the service more intimate. His New York visits inspired him to house his own restaurant in a similar venue.

After working in Florida under the watchful eye of one of the nation's most respected chefs, Trotter began the final leg of his self-educational odyssey by moving to Paris.

He wasn't going to Paris to attend school or to apprentice in a kitchen, but to wine and dine. For six months, he sampled the sumptuous fare and experienced the exquisite service in the city that invented haute cuisine. He studied the lives of the great chefs and read their cookbooks.

TO THE MOUNTAINTOP

The crowning moment of Trotter's grand tour occurred at Girardet in Crissier, Switzerland, where legendary chef Fredy Girardet presided until his 1996 retirement. It was a magical moment for Trotter, who realized "that enough was enough." It was time for him to bear down on his dream after having experienced the best restaurant on the planet. He was struck by how Girardet masterfully orchestrated the cuisine, the wine, the ambiance, and the service. Those four elements would become the pillars of his own restaurant that he and his father opened in August 1987, a month before his twenty-eighth birthday.

"No one of those four elements do we consider more important than the other," says Trotter, who's ever mindful of how a poorly served meal can overshadow the kitchen's and the sommelier's best efforts, not to mention the damage it can cause to the restaurant's reputation. And no one knows that better than the restaurant's servers, who are acutely aware that the 125 guests who visit the restaurant five nights a week are anticipating a monumental dining experience.

"Because the reviews have been so glowing, the guests' expectations are very high," says Jason Platt, a server. "Some people might be looking for a flaw in our service." For some, the visit to Charlie Trotter's is a once-in-a-lifetime event, perhaps a fiftieth birthday or a twenty-fifth wedding anniversary. Other guests may have flown to Chicago specifically to visit the famed restaurant. Another guest may be hosting an important business client and hope to impress the client with a well-chosen venue. Still other guests—call them foodies—frequently dine at the restaurant and have come, like the rest of the guests, to expect a perfectly executed evening.

CHALLENGED BY THE GUESTS

With a clientele like that, the pressure is on the service team to perform like it's the seventh game of the Word Series—every night. "Our clients can be demanding, and that's fine," says Trotter. "We like demanding guests. They bring out the best in us."

Trotter encourages his staff to dine out as often as they can—be it a casual dining establishment or a fine dining restaurant—so they get a sense of having the shoe on the other foot. He wants them to empathize with the people they are serving. Bank, hotel, retail, and airline managers can encourage their service employees to do the same. Become a customer to discover how you would like to be treated. See life from the other side.

At the first preservice meeting after the restaurant had been closed for a two-week break, Trotter asked each server to describe a dining experience during his or her vacation. Most of the service staff expressed disappointment in the way they were treated at the various restaurants. One server was appalled by how unfamiliar the server was with the food. It was as if the server was simply delivering the goods, sight unseen. Indifferent, uncaring, and flawed service seemed to be the norm. Then again, these disciples of Charlie Trotter, whose nightly marching orders are to do whatever it takes to satisfy a customer, have come to expect an almost impossibly high standard of service.

PUTTIN' ON THE RITZ

Trotter's service staff may be a bit spoiled. While the elegant, carefully maintained trappings, the state-of-the-art equipment, and the unique foodstuffs are ultimately to impress the guest at Charlie Trotter's, the investments in such quality and the attention to detail are not lost on the staff.

They note the enormous expense, for example, of opening up to sixty bottles of wine for tasting at training sessions or the cost of having two sommeliers on staff or the unusually high ratio of service staff members to the number of guests served. "These are not the kinds of things that would be done at a restaurant that was finance driven," says Kevin Cronin, a server who's worked at such places. "The goal here is to make the guests extremely excited about being here and blown away by the experience."

Marvin Godinez, who coordinates the restaurant's team of server assistants and food runners, says there are plenty of perks, but the best reward is hearing a customer tell him that he or she has just enjoyed the dining experience of a lifetime. "That tells me we have accomplished our goal," he says.

A SIGHT FOR SORE EYES

Achieving that goal would not be possible without an infrastructure of the best that money can buy. In the kitchen are custom-made French Bonnet stoves with solid brass hinges, pieces of original artwork to make the environment more pleasant, and smoke-eating vents built into a stainless ceiling that purify the air and remove the grime. Only the world's most discerning food purveyors supply the kitchen. Below, the restaurant's wine cellars are meticulously maintained. They are truly showrooms, not just storage bins.

In the dining rooms, meals are presented on the finest china and the wine is served in pristine crystal stemware. Colorful bouquets accent each dining room. Every inch of the restaurant is as spotless as the crystal, and when something breaks or burns out, it's quickly repaired or replaced.

The investments in quality don't come at the employees' expense; they are rewarded with one of the industry's top compensation packages, including health benefits, vacation time, and a retirement plan. The staff are trained to the hilt and treated like professionals.

WORKING WITH THE BEST

"People know that they are going to have the best things to work with here," says Trotter. "If the equipment is treated with respect, employees know they will be able to do a better job. I think they also realize that they have a boss who cares enough to buy the best so they can work at the top of their game.

"To succeed, you need to be surrounded by the best people, the best equipment, the best-maintained equipment, the best product, the best customers, the best of everything." But the best of everything doesn't come easy. "You have to earn the best of everything every single day," says Trotter. "You have to earn the best customers coming in the door. You have to earn the best employees willing to come to work with you. You have to earn the right to have the boss give you the best new equipment because of the way you are treating the current equipment.

"You have to earn the right to work with the white truffles and the black truffles and beluga caviar by the way you treat it," he says. "And I think we have that mindset here where fifty-five people have complete respect for everything around them. They are earning the right every day to continue earning these great opportunities. They take nothing for granted."

> "Working at the finest restaurant on the planet is an honor. I get to work with the best. We are at our best when we pay attention to the little details."
>
> *Ari Kastrati, server*

Of his fifty-five employees, twenty-five have been with the restaurant from five to fourteen years. "They are the unofficial archivists or reviewers of the policies. They can point things out to the newer employees and remind them that it's not always done with such attention to detail at other restaurants."

The staff are excited and motivated when they see the restaurant put something back into the business such as refurbished or upgraded equipment and expansions such as a new $350,000 studio kitchen or a new wine cellar. They realize that they have a stake in the business being profitable; their hard work produces those exceptional results. They're working for more than just a paycheck.

GOD IS IN THE DETAILS

"I don't think people want to work in an environment where a scratched chair or a broken door goes ignored. If there is something wrong with the floor, our attitude is not to find the cheapest way to fix it but to repair it in the best way possible. We're not concerned about the cost."

Trotter has enjoyed some splendid meals in other restaurants. But what he can't stomach is the frequent lack of care for the fine points. Chipped seat backs, cracked plates, and shopworn carpeting seem to be tolerated at even some of the best restaurants. But Trotter believes that guests notice those seemingly insignificant details, and so do the employees.

"The staff notices when the little things begin to slip. It could be as simple as a light bulb that's not been replaced, but it can be demoralizing," says Dan Fitzgerald, dining room manager. Guests are just as aware. "The whole evening is an accumulation of small details. That's why we check the restroom after each guest. Water could be splashed on the floor or a towel could be on the ground when the next guest walks in," says Fitzgerald.

SWEATING THE SMALL STUFF

Ironically, doing the little things costs a company nothing, yet few companies are willing to do them, says Fitzgerald, who has worked in several sectors of the service industry. Companies are more efficient when they do the little things right; the employees are more content and the customers are more satisfied. But it's easier said than done, says Fitzgerald, who once tried to apply the Trotter rules to another business. But it all fell on deaf ears. The mindset simply wasn't there.

People have to buy into the mindset, he says. After his first stint in the mid 1990s at Trotter's, Fitzgerald says he developed a keen eye for detail, a condition he shares with nearly all of his fellow Trotter employees. Addressing a flaw, and doing it quickly rather than waiting for the next person to do something about it, is second nature.

Trotter says attention to the minutiae is the glue that holds the entire dining package together. All along the way, the details have to be tended to—from the first contact on the phone, to how the guest is greeted at the curb, to how the guest is brought into the restaurant, to the presentation of the menu, to the service of the food and wine. And if all those steps are done right, then the guest should have no problem paying for a dining experience that would otherwise seem ridiculously expensive.

"But if you think of it in terms of cost per hour, perhaps $50 to $60 an hour, then you realize what an absolute bargain it is. You can't see a doctor or a lawyer or an accountant for anything close to that," says Trotter.

"In exchange for their $50 to $60 an hour, you have a team of forty-five people, many who are experts in their field and many who have been honing their craft for more than ten years, who are pouring their skill and their time into this dining experience," he says. "The guest is eating off exquisite plateware, picking up beautiful flatware, and sipping from $25 stems while being cared for by people who are charming, knowledgeable, and experts in the service field. The guest is getting a pretty good deal. We've had people tell us that they've been dining out for years but this was the best experience they ever had in their life. It seems cheap at $150 to $160."

SERVICE POINTS

To keep your staff focused on the customers and the small details that won't go unnoticed, keep these service points in mind:

- Have your employees walk in the customer's shoes by patronizing similar businesses.

- Ask yourself: "How would I like to be treated if I were the customer?"

- Respect demanding customers; they can bring out the best in you and your staff.

- Seek inspiration by visiting the leading company in your field.

- Don't mistake service for servitude.

- Be mindful of how damaging poorly rendered service can be to your business.

- Invest in your employees as you would your equipment; develop appropriate compensation.

- Invest in high-quality equipment and supplies. They are tangible reminders to employees that your business wants the best.

- Tend to the little things. Employees will learn that attention to small and large matters is equally important.

2

Reading the Customer's Mind

Too many businesses are content when their service staff is merely competent. But that's not good enough at Charlie Trotter's, where the staff not only treats its guests with great respect but anticipates their needs to create an extraordinary dining experience for some of the toughest customers in the business.

A successful experience in a restaurant—or any business—begins with a good experience with the service representatives: the staff. Charlie Trotter says a business can't succeed until it identifies exactly how it wants its service staff to treat the customer. Trotter's service philosophy is pretty simple: Treat the customer like you would like to be treated. With that philosophy as a lodestar, it then becomes a matter of execution.

But what makes a great server or a good customer service rep? At Trotter's, it takes a sense of empathy, a sense of precision, a sense of anticipation, a sense of humor, a sense of clairvoyance, and a sense of priority.

"A good waiter needs to know what needs to be done first," says Mark Signorio, who has trained scores of servers during his many years waiting tables at Charlie Trotter's. "You don't want to get caught up in something that doesn't need to be done at that particular moment. You shouldn't be at the side station getting wine glasses and preparing to open a bottle of wine that's three courses away when the first courses are arriving at your table. You need to be there to describe the dish."

A good server tries to save a step—not take shortcuts—and make smart use of his or her time on the floor to maximize time with a table, explains Signorio. For example, a server working the second-floor dining room has a long way to go to the basement wine cellars. Rather than make two or three separate trips for each bottle of red wine, for example, "I would explain that we serve our reds at room temperature, and I would like to bring all of them up to let them adjust to the room's temperature. I would explain to the guest that they would be able to enjoy the wine at a better temperature. People love that."

KEEN TO THE KITCHEN'S RHYTHM

A good server understands the rhythm of the kitchen, the engine that drives Charlie Trotter's luxury liner. Likewise, service employees should have an innate sense as to how departments outside their own operate. An editorial employee at a publishing firm needs to understand how its production department works, a sales rep for an industrial concern needs to know the ins and outs of his engineering department, and a retailer needs to understand how her company's shipping department works.

"It's not about someone telling you what to do all the time. It's knowing what's coming," says Signorio, noting that he was acutely aware of how the kitchen worked the tables. Once he discerned the pattern for an evening, Signorio could tell with some degree of certainty which table would follow which. "For example, I could watch table 41, which was not in my section, but I would know that table

33, which is in my section, would be next. When table 41 was served, that would be the signal for me to free myself up from one of my tables to be ready for the food to arrive at table 33. I would watch the pattern, rather than be oblivious to it."

Signorio would sometimes stack the deck by turning in all three tickets from his section of the dining room simultaneously so his orders would be in the same block in the kitchen. Food for his tables would then come in a sequence allowing him to stay one step ahead of the game.

Knowing the exact state of the kitchen, says Signorio, "was a trick that I learned to either put out a fire or to blow someone away. I would know that they were cooking risottos and would ask if I could get two mini risottos for table 41. So boom, in thirty seconds you have an extra course at table 41. If they actually had to make the course, it would throw the kitchen off because it takes things out of sequence."

"The idea of dining at Charlie Trotter's is intimidating. The act of dining there, happily, is not. Service is welcoming, friendly, and just formal enough to remind you that you're in the big league. Waiters, as they hand you the menu, deliver a brief introductory explanation of how things work here."

The Chicago Tribune

A GRACEFUL CHOREOGRAPHY

A sense of precision is paramount at Trotter's, which relies heavily on its service as the unifying element of an extraordinary dining experience. Details that might be imperceptible to a guest combine to create a seamless, seemingly effortless performance by the service team.

Dishes are always served from the guests' left and placed gently on the table. To add a touch of flair to the presentation, a team of waiters and food runners will simultaneously place all the plates on a table. Water glasses are never to be less than half filled; tables are cleared with a minimum of clamor created by the clash of flatware; and plates, glasses, and napkins are immediately replaced when a guest gets up from the table. Servers set each table with starched white linens, well-polished stemware, and sparkling china.

Makiko Hattori, who works the restaurant's front door, has refined a technical trick that expedites a guest's departure. By monitoring the restaurant's point-of-sale computer terminal in the foyer-atrium bar, she can reduce the time it takes the valet to bring a departing guest's car to the curb. When a server rings in the desserts for a table, it usually means the guest will be leaving in about a half hour.

Hattori then alerts the valets, who can locate the guests' car and have it warm and waiting at the curb the moment they are ready to leave. This technique has reduced the number of people who would otherwise have to wait ten to fifteen minutes in the foyer-atrium bar. It can become quite congested between the first and second seating around 9 P.M. Guests are especially appreciative of a warm car during the long Chicago winter, says Hattori.

DON'T STEP ON MY PUNCH LINE

Servers bring their own personal touches to the table. Server Debra Torres makes it a point to go immediately to a woman guest at a table. She uses the technique "as a way to break the ice and disarm the whole table." As a woman, she believes she can be more warm than her male colleagues on the floor.

Server Christian Giles has honed his approach to interrupting a conversation at a table. He discussed his technique during a training session that was in part prompted by a complaint from a guest who wrote on a customer satisfaction survey that the server constantly interrupted his table in the restaurant's studio kitchen. "I usually won't walk up to the table and say 'Excuse me,'" said Giles.

"I will move a little closer to the table and catch the eye of a guest who is not talking. That guest, in turn, can get the attention of the person speaking and quiet them." Guests will usually pick up subtle cues that you want to speak to them or to describe a dish, Giles told his fellow service staff members. Servers are taught that it's best to wait a few extra seconds to let a guest finish a story rather than step on his or her punchline.

Gracefully disengaging from a table can be just as difficult, especially from tables with guests who want to pick the server's brain about the food, the wine, the restaurant's history, or Charlie Trotter's background. Guests may even want details about where servers went to college or what they like to do in their spare time. A simple explanation usually carries the day: "I have to help out at another table."

A sense of humor is essential in an environment that can, at least initially, be off-putting to a new guest. "Humor is a prickly area," says Kurt Sorensen, a veteran server who now manages Trotter's To Go. "What might be funny at one table might fall absolutely flat at another." Sorensen says he practices "selective hearing" to get a sense for how lighthearted his conversations can be with a table.

Giles has even added a touch of levity when things don't go quite right. When the restaurant's food runners accidentally switched a dish from the grand menu with one from the vegetable menu, Giles told the table: "We just wanted to give you a taste of what each other are eating tonight." The guests got a laugh out of it and continued to eat what they had been mis-served.

Sommelier Belinda Chang has a way to win over guests. When guests seem particularly taken with a wine or ask to take the empty bottle home with them, she removes the label from the bottle and presents it to the guests before they leave.

Every service staffer likes to give the guest something extra—be it an extra course, an extra glass of wine, assistance making reservations at another restaurant or a jazz club, a tour of the restaurant, or an opportunity to have Charlie Trotter sign a book or a menu for them. These tricks of the trade can convert first-time visitors into loyal customers.

A STEP AHEAD OF THE GUEST

A sense of anticipation is important and practiced in myriad ways at the restaurant. When a guest gets up from a table, a dining room manager who often works the front door will make a beeline for the restroom door and open it for the guest. "The guest will often say how thoughtful that was or 'How did you know?'" The fact is, there aren't many other places the guest could be going at that point. Guidance for the guest is important at Trotter's, where a guest can easily get lost amid the various dining rooms and hallways.

The notion of assisting a guest is so ingrained at Trotter's that a person who visits the restaurant's second-floor corporate offices to pick up a gift certificate or some merchandise will be escorted down the stairs and out the door.

STUFF HAPPENS

But things can go wrong in even the best-run businesses where a dedicated staff has been meticulously trained. Like the night at Trotter's when a food runner accidentally flipped over a tray of twenty amuse courses that tumbled to the kitchen floor. "It was the equivalent of a multicar, chain reaction crash on Lake Shore Drive at 5 o'clock," recalls Sorensen, one of the servers assigned to the large table eagerly awaiting the course.

The twenty people at the table eagerly awaiting their amuse course weren't going to blame the food runner or the kitchen for the nearly twenty-minute delay. They were going to blame Sorensen, who served as the restaurant's ambassador for those guests.

To compensate for the delay, Sorensen lavished extra attention on the table. He apologetically explained that there would be a delay in the delivery of the first course. He feared that he might have twenty angry guests on his hands right from the start, but few at the table seemed to care. Their attention was focused on the restaurant, its ambiance, and what was going on around them. Only one or two people at the table complained to Sorensen about the delay.

THE HEAT IS ON

"As the server, you have to take the heat for delays, many of which you have no control of," says Sorensen. "You just have to smile, be accommodating, and stay focused." Charlie Trotter says complaints about delays between courses surface on the customer satisfaction surveys. The guests will often note that the server did not get food to the table quickly enough for them. But Trotter knows it's usually more complicated than that.

"The customer might say that he or she did not like the dining experience because the service was too slow," says Trotter. "But what they really didn't like was that the kitchen produced the food too slowly. It had nothing to do with the service." But they don't know that and it's the server who catches the flak.

Sorensen says a server's job can be both "unique and enriching and outrageously frustrating. Enriching and outrageously frustrating live right next to each other. You can never be sure when the balance will tip to the point where you want to throw a chair across the room."

Sorensen and the other servers resist the temptation to chuck a chair and maintain a sense of equanimity even in the most challenging of circumstances. Mark Signorio says good servers don't let themselves get unhinged by a difficult guest. "There are some tables that can rattle your cage. You literally feel like quitting, but you have to remember it's only one table. The real professional moves on.

"Service at Charlie Trotter's is orchestrating the grand dining experience for our guests. Service here is tailor-made to each table, based on the individual dynamics of the guests. Some people want you to engage in conversation as part of service. Others may be conducting a business meeting and are not interested in conversation. Service should be comfortable and not overbearing, yet it should be precise and exacting when necessary. Ultimately, service is a hallmark of civilization."

Kurt Sorensen, general manager
of Trotter's To Go

You don't show your distress to another table."

Signorio says that a guest who may be treating a server with hostility or condescension may have an ulterior motive. "Someone who wants to take a lot of the waiter's time by sending plates back to the kitchen on each course to get attention may not be mad at you, but at the person at his or her table."

The hours at Trotter's are long, the stairs are steep, complications are common, the expectations are enormous, and the guests can be demanding, on rare occasions overbearing, obnoxious, or even drunk. Servers have learned to check their egos at the door if they expect to be on top of their game. They have to ride out their own bad moods, illnesses, and personal problems. Waiters hate to wait for things, be it the coffee, the wine, a set of silverware, the food, or the guests themselves, but the delays are often beyond their control.

RESISTING YOUR BEST EFFORTS

But employees that deal with the customer have to roll with the punches and remain focused on the mission of meeting the customer's needs. At Trotter's, the goal is managing an extraordinary dining experience for the guest. There are nights, however, when—try as they will—it's not going to happen. The ultimate frustration, according to Sorensen, "is a table that is not having a good time no matter what you do."

A concierge at Chicago's Four Seasons Hotel managed to make a last-minute reservation at Trotter's for a party of five from Nebraska whose idea of a great dining experience centered around a big steak. But the concierge gave the Nebraskans a bum steer because Trotter's isn't about big slabs of meat. "I tried everything, including adding an extra course," says Sorensen. "But no matter what I did, I couldn't make it happen for them. It was like this dull note in the orchestra. It was the one table in the restaurant that was off."

Working for a boss as demanding as Charlie Trotter, who doesn't hesitate to reprimand an employee either publicly or privately when he or she falls short of his high standards, can be a source of frustration. But the front-of-the-house staffers knew full well what they were getting into when they joined the restaurant with its reputation for obsessive attention to detail and discipline. Trotter is not going to pull any punches with employees who don't meet his standards.

STRIKING A SOUR NOTE

Makiko Hattori says that when Trotter reprimands her for a shortcoming, she doesn't direct her anger at him but at herself. "He once said to me: 'Makiko, you're a classically trained musician. You should be more careful about a detail like that.' And he was right." But even as her self-directed anger simmered, she had to maintain a brave, pleasant face once the guests began streaming through the front door. "Charlie may have just yelled at me, but I still have to act as if I'm having a good day."

Hattori, who played the French horn in one of the top bands at the University of Illinois, likens Trotter to the conductor of an orchestra. The best conductors do not tolerate missed notes or sloppy performances by their musicians. They push their musicians to excel so the entire orchestra soars. "It's no different from running a restaurant. I understand what he is trying to do here," says Hattori.

Another service staff member says she doesn't take it personally when Trotter scolds her for a misstep. "All of us have to realize that there's so much at stake here," she says. A mistake at one level will often snowball into another level of service and end up diminishing the guest's experience.

NO FALSE MOVES

Being a new employee at Trotter's can be frustrating, says Jerry Slater, who had been a dining room manager at another restaurant. Learning a whole new system, especially one as precise as Trotter's, is no easy task. One evening, for example, he was corrected for taking the path of least resistance to retrieve a beverage from behind the bar in the foyer-atrium. The proper route, he was told, was to enter from another side of the bar rather than to try to weave his way through a cluster of guests. On another evening, he was rattled because he couldn't figure out where a wine had been delivered in his dining room. But he noted that those things come with time and training.

One source of frustration, he quickly learned, was that the guests don't always arrive in the best frame of mind because either they or their cab driver or limo driver couldn't find the world-renowned restaurant with a very low profile at the street level. "They're late and it takes them a little time to settle down," says Slater.

Belinda Chang says her first few months as sommelier were difficult because she was unable to spend much time at tables helping guests make choices about wine or providing them information about a producer or a particular vintage. Her load was lightened when Jason Smith, a sommelier at New York's famed 21 Club, was hired as her assistant. But she still feels that she has to spread herself too thin. "Some guests would love to speak to you for hours about wine. It's such a fascinating subject. But the guests understand that I am busy opening and decanting the wine."

A DAUNTING NEW ROLE

Service employees at Charlie Trotter's need to be versatile. Trotter is always looking for ways to flush employees out of their comfort zones. For example, a dining room manager was tapped to coordinate school groups' field trips to the restaurant as part of Charlie Trotter's Culinary Education Foundation. The soft-spoken manager, who acts as a sort of emcee for the twice-weekly events, said he found both the public speaking role and working out the logistics with the private and public schools daunting. But he likes working with the kids and enjoys the idea of giving something back. Those benefits outweigh the frustrations.

And when Trotter encourages an employee to take on an additional role at the restaurant, it's always best to say yes. Trotter, who claims with a chuckle that he couldn't "imagine an easier person to work for than me," says while he may be a tough-minded boss, "I give the employees all the tools that they need to succeed. All they need to do from there is achieve."

There are plenty of frustrations at the restaurant, even one as well-tuned as Trotter's. "You can be positive about them or you can be

"I view service as giving more than what is expected—especially in a friendly, nonobtrusive, and nonpretentious way. By using our sixth sense, knowledge, and creativity, we can guide and assist a guest toward an extraordinary experience. We must be sensitive to a guest's mannerisms and style. Anticipating their needs is key."

Jason Platt, server

negative," says Trotter. "If something is not right, that's OK. Let's work together and fix it, whether it's a problem with the service system or a piece of equipment or a scratched chair. Employees who approach these problems and frustrations from a positive mindset overcome the deficiencies and obstacles and improve the circumstances. By and large, the fifty-five people who work here are optimistic. They recognize that things need to change but they also believe that if they work together they can improve and refine how this restaurant operates."

Trotter looks for a strong, positive spirit in a service employee. That "can-do" quality allows the employee to withstand the rigors of a demanding, customer-focused environment and to take service to the highest level. But to get there, an employee must develop a knack for getting inside the guest's head and anticipating his or her needs.

SERVICE POINTS

To ensure that your service team is delivering an extraordinary experience for customers—even the most demanding ones—keep these service points in mind:

- Develop a keen sense of priority to deliver quality service.

- Use existing technology to refine customer service. Trotter's front-door staff uses its point-of-sale computer to better calculate the time of a guest's departure.

- Employ a sense of humor with customers; when appropriate, it can make a customer's experience more enjoyable and more memorable.

- Understand and observe customer behavior to better anticipate a customer's needs.

- Encourage employees to take the occasional heat from customers, even if the mistake was a coworkers', and resist finger pointing and buck passing.

- Allow employees to apply peer pressure to correct a fellow employee whose performance is dragging down the rest of the team.

- Teach employees that a reprimand is meant as instruction.

PART II

LEADING: HIRING,

MOTIVATING, AND

TRAINING YOUR STAFF

A service-oriented business is only as good as the talent it puts before the customer, which is why Charlie Trotter and his managers are so diligent about making the right hire. Yet he's quick to throw out the rulebook when hiring. Trotter's techniques can be just as unorthodox when it comes to motivating and training service staffers.

3

Help Wanted:
A Passion for Service

Experience is important, but Charlie Trotter looks for more than that. He's looking for passion and sincerity in a potential service employee. Trotter, who estimates he makes the right hire three-quarters of the time, shares the unorthodox techniques he uses to hire—and sometimes rehire—the kind of person who will thrive in the demanding atmosphere of his restaurant.

When an organization has been judged the best in the business, people naturally want to be a member of the team. As one of the most highly regarded restaurants in America, Charlie Trotter's is in the enviable position of cherry picking the very best applicants.

But Charlie Trotter isn't necessarily looking for the most impressive résumé when it comes time to fill a front-of-the-house position. He has hired servers with a world of fine dining experience, some with ten or more years in the business and an array of technical skills. But, he believes in the risk of hiring people with non-traditional backgrounds.

"We often work better with a person who has little or no restaurant experience," says Trotter. "With people like that there's less resistance to change. Sometimes more experienced people are afraid to change." And change is always on the menu at Charlie Trotter's. "That's what's both beautiful and frightening about an independent operation or a small business. You are in the position to make changes, unlike large corporations that have to work through layers of bureaucracy."

Trotter has hired people with average technical skills, but with extraordinary people skills. "We can teach the technical skills, but it's much tougher to teach people skills. We have had servers here that maybe are less than technically superior, and perhaps they miss things like placing the forks in the correct order or they might forget to bring in a champagne glass at the right moment. But they are so genuinely caring and personable at the table that it more than compensates for their technical imperfections. The larger question is 'What's the greatest good for the guest?' That's why we're sometimes willing to forgo the technical touch for the caring touch."

Businesses that restrict their hiring to candidates with specific industry experience may be overlooking a future star. Trotter has taken some risks by hiring from outside his industry, but in most cases they've paid off by bringing into the fold employees who are intensely customer focused.

HIRING FOR PASSION

When hiring, Trotter puts a premium on such qualities as enthusiasm, dedication, and commitment. He's also looking for someone with the physical, emotional, and mental stamina that will allow him or her to concentrate at a high level for long periods in a demanding, supersonic atmosphere. In short, he's looking for someone like himself.

When interviewing job candidates, Trotter's style is as improvisational as his cooking. "I don't use a script or a set of questions. It's more like a conversation. I might ask them what they're reading, what their favorite movie was, what they like to do in their spare time, what they can contribute here, what they want to accomplish in the next couple of years, and why they want to be here. I want to know what makes them tick."

A red flag in the interview for Trotter is when a candidate seems preoccupied with title, hours, benefits, and wages. "Those are the kinds of things the right individual won't be focused on at that point. They're all important elements, but I'm not interested in talking about them right off the bat. Those things will take care of themselves."

When a dining room manager asked a candidate why he wanted to work at Trotter's, the interviewee replied that it would look good on his résumé. Wrong answer. Certainly a stint at Trotter's looks great on a résumé. "It's like getting the equivalent of a Harvard MBA in this field," says Trotter. The Trotter credential has helped launch servers into managerial or consulting positions in the hospitality field. But the candidate's response to the "Why here?" question suggested that the candidate cared more about himself than the restaurant's guests.

Unlike many employers that put on a dog-and-pony show for a job candidate, Trotter presents a warts-and-all depiction of what life will be like for them at the restaurant. "We paint the darkest possible picture," he says. "We tell them about the long hours, the demanding environment, the high expectations, and the intense

> "The service staff are truly passionate about their roles. We have traveled the world and dined in many places, but never have I experienced a staff with such sensitivity and intuition that allow them to anticipate everything that will be needed in the dining room. When we walk in, the staff immediately know our expectations."
>
> *Roxanne Klein, chef-owner of Roxanne's, a raw food restaurant in Marin County, California*

levels of concentration that will be necessary. And if they still want to work here after all that, then that's a good thing because they know exactly what they are getting into. We don't want people to join if they are at all in doubt."

SERVING UP THE RIGHT ANSWER

Trotter invited Makiko Hattori, who had been a marketing representative for a major consumer electronics company, to come in for an interview. Hattori had no restaurant experience, but Trotter recognized a certain spark to her in a brief conversation he had with her one evening after she dined there with her parents. He insisted that she return the next day to speak to him about a job opportunity.

The University of Illinois music major served up a good answer to the "Why here?" question. She explained to Trotter that whether she was working the front desk at the Ritz-Carlton or the front counter at McDonald's, her level of enthusiasm for each task would be the same. The response pushed the right buttons with Trotter, who later offered her a front-of-the-house position. "What she said struck me as very natural. It was not something that a job candidate would say just to impress me. I was impressed with her sincerity," he says.

Sincerity, which is essential at Charlie Trotter's, is difficult to drill into a new hire. It's almost imperative to hire sincerity rather than attempt to teach it, says Trotter.

Hattori's hiring was somewhat unorthodox and a bit risky because she had no food service or restaurant experience. She had not even waited tables in college, although she had worked part-time at a hotel in Champaign, Illinois, near the university. But in the course of the interview, Trotter learned that she played the French horn at the concert level, had excelled academically at Illinois, and was genuinely interested in working at the restaurant. He had a gut instinct that she "gets it" and has a service mindset that is similar to his and his staff's.

She was awestruck by the restaurant's rarefied air, the remarkable foodstuffs, and the wait staff's savoir faire. As she was leaving the restaurant with her parents that evening, she approached Trotter and asked him to autograph her menu. "He asked me if I was a student. I told him I had graduated three years ago and that I was working in marketing for Sanyo Corporation. He said 'Would you like to work here?'" It was the start of the conversation that led to her hire.

"Working here is like going to school. It's very exciting. I can't believe I get to do this," says Hattori. "The things that I'm learning here about attention to details and anticipating the customers' needs before they even ask for something are lessons that I could apply to any industry." Hattori says she'd like to parlay her corporate marketing experience and her customer service experience at Trotter's into a career of managing the business affairs of artists. But she says she's in no hurry to leave the front door at Charlie Trotter's.

NO REGRETS ABOUT A CAREER CHANGE

Trotter is always willing to consider a nontraditional candidates for a service staff opening if he senses the person has the right stuff. Kurt Sorensen is an example. He had traveled the country for seven years, consulting companies on how to make their operations safer. One night Sorensen dined at Charlie Trotter's and was smitten with the restaurant's ambiance and the acute attention to detail in both its cuisine and its service. When he learned of an opening on the service staff, he applied. For the next four years, the former safety engineer consulted guests at Charlie Trotter's on how to enjoy a spectacular evening of food and wine. He's glad he made the switch. There's a much more human dimension to serving than to engineering.

When he is on the floor, Sorensen enjoys the interplay with articulate and smartly dressed guests at a table. He's fond of the "level of civilization that's practiced at the restaurant, where twenty chefs work behind the scene, the tables are set with fine china and elegant flatware, and the service staff is well-versed with every element of the evening. I think we take it to a higher level. It may be perceived as old-fashioned, but I hope it never goes out of style."

Sorensen is one of several front-of-the-house staffers who were hired from non–fine dining backgrounds. Trotter isn't terribly concerned about where his employees came from. He's primarily interested in how well they'll perform in the demanding environment of his dining room, where the clientele is sophisticated and the products are complex. New hires can bring a sense of passion and sincerity from any background.

BATTING .750

Trotter estimates that he makes the right call on about three-quarters of his hires. And there have been some hires that struggled mightily in the first six months or more to learn the Trotter service system and philosophy—leading him to wonder whether he hired the right person. But in a number of those cases, the employee grew into the role. "Someone might find that he or she truly has it in them. They have always approached things one certain way before realizing there is a different way to do it. That's exciting when you can help a person open their eyes."

Promising candidates have an audience with Mitchell Schmieding, the restaurant's director of operations and one of the restaurant's first employees. Precise and particular himself, Schmieding will look for telltale signs of sincerity and self-discipline when evaluating a potential employee. If an applicant telephones to ask whether the restaurant is accepting applications, he will routinely say no, but he will invite the applicant to fax him a résumé and cover letter or drop it off at the restaurant's office. He explains to the applicant that he is happy to review a résumé because the restaurant will always consider a qualified applicant when an opening occurs.

"But if I get another phone call from the applicant asking to schedule an interview or asking whether I received their résumé, it tells me that they're not a good listener and don't understand what we are about here," says Schmieding. Another red flag is when the applicant drops by the restaurant with the résumé after 4 P.M., when the restaurant is gearing up for service.

A SENSE FOR SINCERITY

If an applicant is invited in for an interview, it typically takes place in the first floor dining room during the afternoon, prior to service. Schmieding watches for other clues about the person's sincerity during the interview at a dining room table. For example, if the applicant gets up from a table without pushing in his or her chair or fails to help Schmieding clear cups, glasses, or napkins from the table, Schmieding is left to wonder about the person's sincerity, much less his or her serving skills. "A service person with the right instincts would instantly take care of all the debris before we departed because that's what we do. We take care of people."

The interview is not necessarily a good predictor of a candidate's success on the floor. "He or she may look good on paper, speak well, and have all the right answers, but until they spend a night with us you can't be entirely sure," says Schmieding. The length of the shift, which is often ten to twelve hours, sometimes daunts candidates. The pace can be as intense as the emergency room in a big-city hospital.

In the thick of service, some apparently well-qualified candidates demonstrated an inability to open a bottle of champagne or properly serve a plate of food. "A candidate's abilities or lack of them shine through when they're put to the test," Schmieding says. Once the tryout is complete, Schmieding puts the ball in the candidate's court by asking him or her to call back the next day.

PRIMED FOR ROUND TWO

After sleeping on it, some candidates are not heard from again. Those who call the next day and who made a positive impression the night before are invited back for a second interview. Schmieding asks the candidate to return and explain what he or she "expects of us and what we should expect of them if they are hired." He bears down in the second interview by asking a series of open-ended questions, such as: "What did you think of the cuisine? What did you think of the service? and What did you think of your evening with us? If the candidate simply responds that it was great, I probe for a more in-depth answer. I want to get past the superficialities."

Next stop for the candidates is a series of ten- to fifteen-minute interviews with two or three service staff members or a manager. The candidate is encouraged to ask probing questions about the challenges, frustrations, and rewards of working as a service staff member at Charlie Trotter's. After the candidate leaves, Schmieding and the service staff members who met the candidate sit down to discuss the candidate's qualifications and prospects for success if he or she is hired. "If we have a good feeling about the candidate, an offer is extended," he says.

NOT MEASURING UP

He who hires sometimes has to fire. Trotter estimates that he's fired about fifteen employees since the restaurant's 1987 inception. "I hire every employee with an optimistic sense that he or she will succeed. I don't like to give up on an employee. But if an employee is not performing up to standard, I will let them go."

Employees who aren't living up to expectations are put on notice. A manager explains the areas where they are falling short and suggests ways of improving performance. If standards still aren't being met, the employee is given a final warning. If the employee is still found wanting, the employee is shown the door. In some cases where an employee's performance has been substandard, Trotter or a manager will turn up the heat on an employee. Such employees may then recognize they're not cut out for the position and quit on their own. Dismissal is immediate for an employee who comes to work under the influence of drugs or alcohol. An employee who mistreats a guest can also be dismissed on the spot.

Trotter once had to fire a server who seemed more interested in socializing with the guests than serving them. "He was a social butterfly," says Trotter, noting that there's a place for conviviality but not at the expense of service. The last straw was when the server abandoned his station to march bread across the room to the table of a movie star. Celebrities, who frequent the restaurant, are handled in a quiet manner to respect their privacy. Trotter has a strict policy of not publicizing the names of the rich and famous who dine at his restaurant.

On another occasion, Trotter fired one of his managers who had requested a couple of days off on short notice. Trotter turned him down saying that he absolutely had to have him on duty those days. The manager responded by saying that he was taking the time off regardless. When he returned after the two-day absence, Trotter told the manager he was through.

"It's never fun to fire an employee," says Trotter. "I try to do it the least painful way possible." The ugliness of a firing, of course, can often be avoided by hiring the right person in the first place.

THE HAVES AND THE HAVE-NOTS

Some have it and some don't. One who does is Makiko Hattori, who unconsciously displayed her natural flair for service within days of her hiring. A dining room manager recalls how Hattori instinctively cleared a table in the dining room as she was walking toward the restaurant's back door at the end of her shift.

"It's 11:30 at night and she's ready to go home. A lot of people would say good night and walk out the door. But as she was walking out, she noticed that table 22 was not cleared. She took care of everything. You can have people who have worked here for years and will walk through a dining room and not notice glasses that need to be cleared from a table or a napkin that needs to be replaced. She has the kind of instincts that let a person see things happening on the floor before they actually develop."

An engineer's eye for precision and detail, says Sorensen, has served him well at Charlie Trotter's, where the tolerances can be as tight as an engineering design. He believes that a career as a server—or any food professional—is every bit as important and intellectually stimulating as that of an engineer. "I've heard someone say that not many people aspire to be a waiter," says Sorensen. "I couldn't help but laugh under my breath. If only they knew what we had to do. I'm convinced we could step into the shoes of just about anyone because we are so used to adapting to many different work environments at the drop of a hat."

NEW CHALLENGES IN A NEW VENUE

Debra Torres returned to the server ranks after rising to the position of general manager at Spruce, a three-star Chicago restaurant. She hardly thinks she's moving in the wrong direction on the career ladder because managing tables and learning the food and wine at Charlie Trotter's are every bit as challenging as running a restaurant.

The stigma attached to waiting tables—that it's only a job to pay the bills for school or to support an artistic career—is unfair, certainly at a fine dining restaurant like Trotter's. "You have to be incredibly focused on food and wine just as an attorney would have to be focused on the law. It takes the same level of professional commitment." She says actors or dancers or artists do not wait tables at Trotter's because the fifty- to sixty-hour workweek would leave them little time to pursue their muse.

Torres, who would like to be considered for a managerial position at Trotter's after she masters her role as server, says that besides the restaurant's world-class wine program, the biggest reward "is working in a culture with such a strong sense of discipline. It's a great foundation for character building that will permeate throughout my life. With so many people with the same agenda here, how could someone not succeed?"

AN ENCYCLOPEDIC BREADTH OF KNOWLEDGE

A server at Charlie Trotter's needs to be conversant with a cornucopia of exotic foodstuffs that appear on two constantly changing tasting menus. A server must be confident enough to handle a fifty-five-page wine list with more than 1,500 selections. And the server must also be able to finesse a variety of situations at the table and throughout the dining room.

In addition, a good server needs to have the confidence to occasionally negotiate matters with and make suggestions to the chefs in the kitchen. Sorensen has assisted with service for the King of Sweden's visit to the restaurant's famed kitchen table, corporate meetings, weddings, and other special occasions at the restaurant. When assigned to the kitchen table, a server becomes an entire service team rolled into one. As the server, server assistant, food runner, and sommelier, the person assigned to the kitchen table must orchestrate the twelve- to thirteen-course meal.

Like a good concierge, a server needs to know the lay of the land. Local and out-of-town guests often call on their server to make recommendations on clubs, cultural attractions, and other restaurants. Because Trotter gives front-of-the-house staffers enormous discretion to ensure that everything at a table is flawless, servers have to be focused and quick on their feet. A split-second decision could make or break an evening for a guest. "There is always so much going on in your mind as you try to handle the various demands of a station. It's hard to keep it all straight."

Sorensen convinced Trotter that he could make the transition from engineering to serving because "I have an innate sense of service. I feel very comfortable doing it. I feel that I should be helping people. Charlie Trotter has always said that service is not servitude, and I agree with that. I think service is a career."

Trotter has contributed to his service team's sense of professionalism by putting them on a salary-like compensation and benefits program, doing away with uniforms in favor of dark suits, and meeting with the front-of-the-house staff each day before service. As a result, turnover is low.

A GAMBLE THAT PAID DIVIDENDS

Belinda Chang says Charlie Trotter's always intrigued her, and she had vowed to pay a visit. She did so during her senior year at Rice University in Houston when she was back in her hometown of Chicago during a break from school. "I had read so much about the restaurant. It

"Service is anticipation; needs should be met before the guest realizes that they have arisen. It's going the extra mile and providing guests with more than what they think they need. It's having all the information and knowing all the answers or knowing how to get them for a guest. It's timing; it benefits both the restaurant and the guest. It's comfort; every guest should have what he or she needs to be comfortable. It's desire; a great server wants to provide whatever it takes to make the guest's experience the very best."

Belinda Chang, sommelier

sounded fascinating to me." Unfortunately her parents and friends whom she hoped to enlist for a visit didn't share her fascination. They said the price of an evening at Charlie Trotter's was too rich for their taste.

So Chang went alone. Admitting that she was completely clueless, she showed up at 4:30 P.M. On weeknights, however, service doesn't begin until 6 P.M. "I could see the silver being polished, and the waiters were holding their preservice meeting," she recalls. Nevertheless, several service people made her feel welcome as she awaited her first meal at Charlie Trotter's. The experience, she says, more than lived up to her expectations. She wrote a letter to Trotter telling him how much she enjoyed the experience and how much she wanted to work at his restaurant.

Trotter, who was impressed with Chang's letter, wrote her back expressing his thanks for her interest in working at the restaurant, but he didn't have an opening. When a friend in Chicago saw a classified newspaper ad for a server position at Trotter's a month later, Chang applied and was invited to interview. Trotter took a chance on a recent college graduate, but the gamble paid off. Chang quickly became a favorite among the guests due in large part to her sincerity and her command of food and wine.

Less than two years after her July 1997 hiring, Trotter invited her to begin training as a sommelier. Chang recalls that she had not requested the position. "He said, 'I think this would be good for you. Would you be interested in training as a sommelier?' Of course, I said yes."

She was delighted, although she was not certain she was up to the challenge. Charlie Trotter's has a rich legacy of wine service. Two of its former sommeliers have won the world sommelier competition—the only Americans to earn the honor. Chang began educating herself on wine, reading voraciously and tasting the wares of the wine distributors who regularly visit the restaurant. She earned her certification from the Grand Court of Master Sommeliers and is studying for the designation of Master Sommelier. "One of the great things about working here is that staff members are exposed to many interesting events. It's a continuing education."

For example, Chang attended Christie's millennium event in New York City and worked an extravagant dinner at the chateau of a Canadian wine collector, who won a charity auction bid to have Charlie Trotter and some of his chefs prepare a special meal in his home. At the dinner, Chang sampled some fifteen rare bottles of Bordeaux from his wine cellar. "That's what is so exciting about this place. There's always a wine I don't know or a foodstuff that I've never seen before. It's a challenge to do all the reading and research necessary to keep up. It's important for me to be at events here and at other cities because with wine, it's all about what you have tasted, and that helps you translate it for the guest."

Once a week, wine distributors visit the restaurant, and Chang meets with each rep during fifteen-minute sessions. She tastes at least sixty wines that day and talks with the representatives about the attributes of each wine.

GOOD WITH NUMBERS AND MORE

Mitchell Schmieding began working at the restaurant in 1988 while studying for his certified public accounting (CPA) exam. He had managed several suburban Chicago restaurants prior to joining Trotter's. Bob Trotter, the chef's late father, was looking for someone with an accounting and management background to help him manage the restaurant's financial affairs.

Schmieding's responsibilities grew, and he now plays several roles at the restaurant including training and supervising the front-of-the-house staff. Endowed with a green thumb, he is also the restaurant's official gardener. During the evening he helps orchestrate service by floating through the dining rooms and the foyer-atrium bar. He typically works a swing shift, applying his skills in the restaurant's office in the afternoons and working in the dining room at night. He says he much prefers juggling his various roles at Charlie Trotter's to working at an accounting firm or a corporation because "I wasn't sure I wanted to spend my career sitting at a steel desk under a fluorescent light."

THE BOOMERANG FACTOR

A dozen of the restaurant's fifty-five employees are on their second tour of duty. Trotter likes to rehire talented former employees. "They bring a different mindset back with them because they have been exposed to a less-demanding environment. It makes them better appreciate what we are trying to do here." Employees who leave on good terms and who met the restaurant's high standards while they were there will always be considered for rehiring.

Dan Fitzgerald was the restaurant's assistant dining room manager in 1994 and 1995. He admits that he left because he was burned out from trying to uphold the high Trotter standards night after night. He left the restaurant business and tried his hand at other ventures including a stint in St. Petersburg, Russia, working for a company that provides services—from limousines to bodyguards—for American businesspeople.

Contemplating a return to the United States, Fitzgerald e-mailed Trotter and asked whether Trotter would serve as a reference for him. Trotter replied that the next time Fitzgerald was in the United States, he would like him to visit to talk about a possible management opportunity at the restaurant. Fitzgerald had planned a visit to Austin, Texas, and agreed to fly to Chicago—on Trotter's nickel—to do some catching up.

In January 2001, Fitzgerald returned to the restaurant business and to Trotter's as a dining room manager to work for the toughest boss he ever had. "He is the most demanding boss, but in a rational way. He will make demands, but unlike other bosses, he will also provide you the resources to meet an objective."

Fitzgerald says he's returned to the business with an enlightened perspective. "I have been a customer for the last five or six years. I think I can better deal with customers because of that." He is excited to again be working at Trotter's. "Charlie Trotter's is the pinnacle of this business. There's no better place that I could be right now."

APPRECIATING THE PAST

Marvin Godinez came back. He joined Charlie Trotter's in 1991 as a server assistant, or what would be known as a busboy at other restaurants. Since his return, he now coordinates a team of ten server assistants and food runners. He typically floats between the kitchen and the dining rooms to ensure that the left hand knows what the right hand is doing.

He left to work as a server assistant in the restaurant of a leading Chicago hotel, but quickly came to appreciate the Trotter touch when he experienced a restaurant that was not nearly as diligent about its quality of service. He would sometimes complain to supervisors or colleagues at the restaurant about haphazard practices or conditions by noting that they would not be tolerated at his former restaurant. "I would try to tell them how we did certain things at Charlie Trotter's," says Godinez. "But the typical response was: 'We're not Charlie Trotter's.'" Disheartened by the restaurant's comparatively lackadaisical standards, Godinez reapplied at Charlie Trotter's, where the work is hard, the boss is tough, and the clientele is demanding but the floors are always clean.

As the old song goes, it's hard to keep 'em keep down on the farm once they've seen Parée.

SERVICE POINTS

Decisions on hiring, rehiring, and sometimes firing service staffers are among the most critical a manager will make. Consider these service points when making those tough calls:

- Hire for passion, enthusiasm, and sincerity, not just for experience.

- When interviewing a job candidate, don't work from a script; make it a conversation.

- Focus less on skills and experience and more on what animates the candidates, e.g., favorite books or movies or what a candidate does in his or her spare time.

- Pose questions or watch for telltale signs that speak to a candidate's level of sincerity about a job.

- Ask open-ended questions, but don't settle for superficial responses. Push the candidate to provide thoughtful, genuine responses.

- Have a candidate interview or be interviewed by potential colleagues. Ask the employees for their impression of the candidate.

- Turn up the heat on underperforming employees. They will either respond to the increased pressure to perform or realize they aren't suited for the job.

- Rehire talented former employees. They return with a renewed sense of purpose and desire to perform at your quality establishment.

- Invest in employees; take them to events outside the office to enhance their skills and their understanding of the industry.

4

Stoking the Fires of Passion

How do you light a fire under an employee? Steal a page from Charlie Trotter, who has one of the most motivated service staffs in the industry. He doesn't like the term *motivation,* preferring to inspire his staff through empowerment, his own example of passionately striving to be the best, and with a variety of offbeat techniques. Charlie Trotter believes that if he has to motivate an employee he has hired the wrong person.

"Motivation is not my job," Trotter told a group of wide-eyed high school students gathered in his studio kitchen one afternoon to learn about excellence. "My staff need to motivate themselves. Self-motivation is the best way to ensure top performance. Employees need to make sure that their own standards are higher than their boss's."

But Trotter is not shirking what would seem to be one of his most important responsibilities as chef-owner of the fifty-five-employee restaurant. "I don't believe in management. I have no time for it. But I am very interested in leadership."

DO AS I DO

He leads by example. Employees can watch firsthand each night as he applies his meticulous touch to everything in the house—from designing an intricate dish to inspecting the restaurant's stemware for signs of a blemish. No task is beneath him. He's hauled garbage, answered the front door, run food to tables, and toted armloads of cookbooks from one end of the building to the other. Intense, focused, and energetic, Trotter tackles large and small matters with equal care and enthusiasm.

The environment at Charlie Trotter's is inspirational. The tables are set with fine china and delicate Reidel crystal stemware, and the wine is drawn from carefully constructed cellars housing a $1 million–plus collection. The food is prepared in a state-of-the-art kitchen that was remodeled in 1998 at a cost of more than $750,000. A new hire will find himself or herself on a fast track. Front-of-the house employees, like their colleagues in the kitchen, are some of the best in the business.

Employees take their cues from their indefatigable leader. Trotter typically works a twelve-hour day, beginning in his second-floor office around noon and ending after midnight (service often doesn't end until 1 A.M.) in the restaurant's state-of-the art kitchen where he scrutinizes every dish headed for the dining room. But there is no typical day for him. Some days begin as early as 8 A.M. when he's in production in the restaurant's studio kitchen for *The Kitchen Sessions with Charlie Trotter.* He's an entrepreneur by day and a chef by night.

His days off can be even busier. The restaurant is closed on Sundays and most Mondays, which allows him to travel on those days for media appearances, speeches to college students, and culinary events, or to host special events sponsored by his restaurant. Although he's reduced his travel schedule from his earlier days, travels with Charlie can be exhausting. On a trip to New York, he began the day with an appearance on NBC's *Today Show,* followed by an interview on the Television Food Network. Next it was on to Bloomberg radio. He then took his staff members that had accompanied him to New York to lunch. He next hosted a three-hour cooking demonstration at Macy's and later met people from the culinary field for dinner. He flew back Tuesday morning and was at his post in the kitchen that night.

Fortunately, he has the stamina of a well-conditioned athlete. A gymnast in high school, Trotter has maintained an athletic regimen. On his fortieth birthday, he ran a marathon in France. He performs calisthenics and regularly takes less ambitious runs near his home to remain fit and trim, unlike those middle-aged chefs who are unable to resist the temptations of the kitchen.

BE LIKE MIKE

Trotter has long admired the athleticism and leadership of Michael Jordan, whose work ethic and drive to excel inspired his Chicago Bulls teammates to play an exceptional game. "I don't think Jordan ever said that it was his job to motivate his teammates," says Trotter. "I think he was saying that he simply had to be the best and the others would follow. In turn, Scotty Pippin might do something spectacular that would only add fuel to the fire."

Trotter was mentioned in the same vein several years ago when *Chicago* magazine named the meanest Chicagoans. Jordan was first, Trotter second. The article cited Trotter's obsessive quest for excellence and quoted him as saying: "When you come to work at Charlie Trotter's, you basically give up your life to the pursuit of perfection."

Personal sacrifice, he believes, is essential to professional and personal success. He cites Russian novelist Feodor Dostoevski's belief that young people should resign themselves to giving up five years of their lives to lay the groundwork for their careers. Trotter does not necessarily ask for a five-year commitment from his young

employees, but he does challenge them to work with a high level of
passion for a demanding, sometimes sharp-tongued boss, a discriminating clientele, and in an atmosphere that demands perfection.

TURNING UP THE HEAT

Chicago's second-meanest man doesn't hesitate to get in employees' faces when he suspects they're giving less than their best.
Employees know better than to test Trotter's temper, which some
say has mellowed with age. "Believe me, I still know how to motivate the hell out of everyone who works here," says Trotter in
response to a question about his occasionally heavy-handed motivational techniques. "But I'm not sitting up late at night thinking
about how I'm going to motivate these guys."

The best motivational technique, as far as he's concerned, is "to
set a certain tone that is established through how I conduct myself.
I motivate myself and the managers who have been deputized to be
leaders motivate," says Trotter. "Even those who have not been des-
ignated as leaders can motivate. And when they do, it creates a
synergy or electricity in this restaurant. Someone can do something
so inspirational that it has a domino effect."

Employees are motivated, Trotter believes, by "the fact that we're
trying to do everything here at such a high level." Trotter and his
staff's quest for excellence has not been lost on the media and the culinary community, which has showered accolades on the restaurant.

SKEWERED BY THE CRITICS

The applause for Trotter's can be inspirational but so can the criticism. In March 1999, *Chicago* magazine dropped its rating of
Charlie Trotter's from four (its highest ranking) to three and a half
stars. The magazine cited what it called some "overambitious" culinary creations and what it claimed was a slippage in service. The
following month, *Crain's Chicago Business* wrote a front-page story

that reported critics were beginning to wonder whether "the restaurateur-turned-industrialist has spread himself too thin" because of such ventures as Trotter's hot-selling cookbooks, his TV series, and his signing on as a celebrity chef with United Airlines.

Trotter says the stories "made me angry and motivated me to work even harder. I thought the criticism was unfair." Proving that living well is the best revenge, Trotter won the nation's top chef award from the James Beard Foundation the week after the *Crain's* story ran. And a short time after that, *Chicago* magazine restored the restaurant's fourth star, ahead of Charlie Trotter's being named the nation's best restaurant by the James Beard Foundation and by *Wine Spectator*. Amid the criticism, Trotter says he never doubted that the restaurant and its staff were still at the top of their game.

He says his anger over the stories was tempered by the fact that the restaurant had already established a strong twelve-year track record. "Stories like that would have been far more damaging if we were only a year or two old," says Trotter, who's well aware that when you hang your name on the door you have to take the good with the bad.

FINDING INSPIRATION THROUGH BEAUTY

To keep his restaurant running at a championship level, Trotter uses a variety of unconventional motivational techniques, including showing his service staff movies that he considers to be artfully produced. His favorites include *Apocalypse Now*, the movie about the madness of the Vietnam war directed by Francis Ford Coppola, and *Fitzcarraldo,* directed by German filmmaker Werner Herzog. "I show the staff these movies so they can see the beauty of how something is done, how passion can lead to an outstanding production."

He says, "*Fitzcarraldo* is especially motivating because it's the story of a man with the quixotic dream of bringing opera to the Amazon by dragging a boat over a mountain. It's a story of sheer

"Good service does not mean performing well or treating a customer well only when you are getting paid well. It means performing well regardless of how much you are going to make from a particular customer. If you are a service professional, you should take pride in doing the best possible job and treating customers as well as possible—at all times. Because that is what you are: a professional."

Dan Fitzgerald,
dining room manager

determination. It shows what dreams are about. Some are so extreme that they are almost unattainable, but that's not all bad."

Trotter likes to take his staff on the road, where they're exposed to other standards of excellence. He's taken his service staff to farms where they can learn about organically raised foodstuffs that the restaurant serves. He's taken staff to New York for wine auctions at Christie's. He took a large contingent to Toronto for a cooking demonstration at a home that boasts one of the world's leading collections of wine from the Bordeaux region of France. He's taken staff to events at Fortune 500 corporations and to events at museums in Chicago and New York.

REACHING FOR THE BRASS RING

Working in an atmosphere where excellence is the norm can be inspirational, albeit a bit intimidating. Kevin Cronin, a server, says the expectations are enormous. "To be successful here you have to have a passion and genuine interest in the food and wine. There is a level of commitment required at this restaurant that is much higher than at just about any other restaurant. Our knowledge of food is certainly higher."

To maintain the restaurant's brass-ring standards, Cronin says he feels compelled to continually educate himself by reading every food magazine and cookbook he can get his hands on. One of the benefits of the job is the exposure to the best of everything in the culinary world. "But it's a challenge here because things are constantly changing," says Cronin. "The briefings by the chefs during preservice meetings can't possibly cover it all." Sophisticated and just plain curious diners toss questions at the servers, who are expected know the finer points of each dish.

But Cronin isn't complaining about the high standards because he's waited tables at restaurants where the overriding concern was the bottom line. "They were very finance driven, at least from the owner's perspective," he says. "Whereas here the goal is to make the guests extremely excited about being here and being thrilled by the experience."

Employees will chide colleagues whose self-motivation has slipped a notch, says Kurt Sorensen. "The esprit de corps is strong. There's almost a tribal sense of management. If someone is not pulling their weight, we let them know. None of us has a problem telling a colleague to get going because nothing is below anyone, including Charlie Trotter, whom I've seen clear tables or bring food to tables. That's the way it should be."

SUMMONING AN INNER STRENGTH

Working at Trotter's not only takes a high level of mental concentration to properly juggle all the tasks but requires physical stamina as well. The restaurant consists of five dining areas (including the studio kitchen and the famed kitchen table) on three floors spread across two adjoining buildings. Burnout can be a problem, especially by Saturday night, the last night of the workweek. "That's where the fat cells come in," says Rene Roman, a server who transferred to a cook's position in the kitchen. "You have to psych yourself up mentally some nights. I think of it as a performance. You have to know your lines. There's no place to hide on the floor."

Roman says "knowing your lines" entails knowing what's on
the menu, knowing what's on the wine list and what's not, and
being aware of all sorts of countless items that a guest may inquire
about. It also means consistency, doing the job at the highest possible level, night after night after night. If a service team member
shows signs of slowing down, he or she will hear about it, not from
Trotter, but from his or her coworkers. "We get on each other if we
have to," says Roman.

Debra Torres says the toughest times at the restaurant for her are
when things hit a lull. She says she has no problem maintaining an
intense focus for long periods when the pace is brisk, particularly on
Friday and Saturday nights. During a lull, though, she can feel herself losing her edge and asking herself, "What should I do next?"
But most nights, especially the weekends, are exhilarating. "You
have to be smart and fast and be able to respond to every possible
situation at any given moment. This place is like the Japanese bul-
let train. It's fast, it's sleek, it's a remarkable creature."

Dan Fitzgerald says rallying the troops is much tougher to do
on Tuesday when everyone has returned from the weekend than on
Saturday when the finish line is in sight and the adrenaline is running high. "The big challenge is trying to get people excited every
single night. It's tough sometimes getting everybody back in gear
on Tuesday."

GUARDING AGAINST COMPLACENCY

If colleagues don't get to an employee who has put it on autopilot,
Trotter certainly will. He's noticed that many employees tend to
plateau after a year on the job, perhaps feeling they've conquered
the challenges of their first 365 days. "Even the most intelligent
and ambitious people will find a level they are comfortable with,"
he says. "One of the hardest things a leader or a visionary has to do

is set a tone that will serve as an incentive and keep people from falling back on something they are comfortable with."

There's the risk that the entire restaurant could level out. "It's easy to say the guests were happy. They gave us all 5s on the customer satisfaction surveys. We're making a profit, and we've achieved critical success. So why rock the boat?"

But Trotter says he's going to continue to push himself and his staff to be their best. "Can we do a better job? The answer is yes because we are still a relatively young restaurant. We have a ways to go. We can always say we could have done a better job at this table. We could have better customized it. It's a matter of never being satisfied with what we do."

SHOW ME THE MONEY

Trotter's service team is not only highly motivated, it is well paid. However, servers at Charlie Trotter's aren't working their tables for tips. They're working for a regular paycheck.

In a departure from industry practice, service team members at Charlie Trotter's are paid every other Wednesday. The annual compensation for servers, which ranges from $40,000 to $80,000 a year, is based primarily on experience and their sales averages for the previous few years. Compensation is also influenced by how well servers score on customer satisfaction surveys that about 70 percent of the diners fill out. Trotter realizes, however, that complaints about a server's slow service may actually be the kitchen's fault or due to other circumstances beyond the server's control.

Front-of-the-house staffers also receive health and dental insurance, paid vacation, and a 401(k) plan. The restaurant is closed about three weeks a year, and employees schedule their vacations at that time. Employees can invest up to 15 percent of their salary in the 401(k) program, and Trotter's will match 25 percent of their contributions. Employees are eligible for annual merit-based raises, salary bonuses for exemplary service, and promotion to manager status; the top supervisors earn about $120,000. Benefits, not to mention a regular wage, are the exception for front-of-the-house employees in a business where the rule of thumb is cash-and-carry.

CASH IS NO LONGER KING

Charlie Trotter's compensation plan is part of an effort to professionalize the ranks of its front-of-the-house staff. The plan has more than paid for itself; Trotter has been able to attract more career-minded staffers who tend to reward Trotter with their longevity. A majority of the front-of-the-house staff have been at the restaurant more than five years, which is an eternity in the notoriously flighty restaurant industry. Turnover among customer service staffers at any business can be debilitating. And too many service-focused companies tend to be penny-wise and pound-foolish when it comes to maintaining and motivating staff that work directly with the customer.

Promoting longevity translates into more consistent, more knowledgeable service for the guest. Those who visit the restaurant on a regular basis will often ask to be seated at their favorite server's station. Trotter's won't always accommodate such a request so guests can experience service at the hands of other team members as well.

Trotter, who began his career as a busboy and then a waiter, said taking home my "dirty wad of cash each night was one of the grubbier aspects of the job. I would rather have received a paycheck every two weeks like everyone else that reflected my effort and performance."

The guaranteed wage plan is only one of the key steps Trotter has taken to upgrade his service staff's status. To further underscore the message that "service is not servitude," Trotter scrapped uniforms in favor of dignified-looking dark suits. He meets with his front-of-the-house staff each day, and he's aggressively trained and educated the staff of food professionals so they can confidently navigate their way through both the dining room and the restaurant's vaunted kitchen.

IT'S LIKE MONEY
IN THE BANK

Kevin Cronin says he much prefers the predictability of a regular paycheck to living off tips each night. "It's great to know what you'll be making. You can pay the bills knowing what you'll be getting in two weeks." At restaurants where servers' compensation is tied strictly to tips, he says waiters can find themselves in a financial pinch after a few slow nights or when they are sent home for a lack of business. A month like January, traditionally the slowest in the restaurant industry, can leave a server hard-pressed just as the bills from the holidays come pouring in.

"Trotter's is equal of any Michelin three-star restaurant in Europe or the best restaurants in New York. Charlie has done a great job of breaking down the barriers between the kitchen and the front-of-the-house staff. He's got the entire team focusing on the customer's dining experience. It is beautifully integrated."

Ray Harris, Wall Street financier who has eaten at Charlie Trotter's nearly 300 times

Judi Carle, the restaurant's controller, said that half the service staff bought homes or condominiums within months after the restaurant switched to regular paychecks. The new compensation plan provides much more stability, says Carle. Banks quickly sign off on mortgage approvals after she sends them a mortgage verification statement. Employees can qualify for car and personal loans more easily also.

There's nothing more stabilizing for an employee than a thirty-year mortgage commitment. The compensation plan also reduces the risk that tax authorities will audit the server. Because servers are paid primarily in cash tips, tax authorities will often audit servers' incomes to ensure that they have accounted for all of their compensation.

Paying servers a regular, biweekly amount rather than having them live hand-to-mouth on tips is manageable at a single restaurant that serves dinner only five nights a week, says Trotter. "I am able to observe each employee every single day. I can make firsthand judgments about each employee's performance. We're still small enough to be able to measure performance subjectively." The compensation plan would, however, become problematic if he were operating a chain of restaurants or a restaurant with two or three shifts of employees, he says. Without personal contact with each employee, it would be more difficult to make compensation assessments. Because Trotter is in the restaurant almost every night, he can personally observe the performance of each employee. Those observations factor into his annual evaluations.

I LIKE WHAT YOU'VE DONE

Wage increases are awarded on a completely sporadic basis, says Trotter. "I might see someone doing a great job and I'll kick it up for him or her. Or there might be a week where I decide to give fifteen people raises—some modest, some substantial. I will write them a note acknowledging their great contributions and encourage them to keep up the great work; here's an expression of my gratitude."

Increases in compensation for the service staff are not tied to their performance evaluations, which are done roughly once a year. "It tends to be fairly spontaneous. I might take a week in the month of March and talk to everyone on the staff for five to thirty minutes. I'll ask: 'How's it going for you? Are you happy? What do you like about your job? What don't you like about your job? What would you like to see done differently?'"

Trotter will then share some observations he's made of the service staff member's performance and make suggestions on how he or she can take it to the next level. The restaurant has tried using standard employee evaluation forms. It's also had employees fill out self-evaluations and match them with the managers' assessments of the employees, but Trotter says, "They're a bit too sterile or too corporate for my taste."

SLACKERS NEED NOT APPLY

Those who argue that fixed incomes will encourage laziness or lack of focus in servers who have lost their incentive for direct tips don't know Trotter. He has no tolerance for slackers on his staff nor would he ever hire one in the first place. Service staff members invariably cite the challenge of using their service skills to exceed the expectations of some of the nation's most sophisticated diners as well as to present some of the world's best foodstuffs and wines as their primary motivation. Money, better yet steady money, helps, of course.

Trotter does not believe that the fixed compensation plan takes money out of the pocket of a hustling, high-energy server who performs at an extraordinary level on a consistent basis. "A server who continues to improve himself or herself will qualify for a higher wage. Instead of $50,000 a year, it could be $60,000 year," he says.

A server's shift begins about two hours prior to service and ends after the last guest leaves. Many nights, the shift is ten hours or more. Servers, perhaps those working their way through college or grad school, who want to earn some quick cash, work a six-hour shift, and be able to swap shifts might not find Trotter's plan appealing. "But we're looking for people concerned about a career. Our plan is appealing to a more mature, more enlightened individual— someone who regards himself or herself as a professional in this field. I think this is a more refined way to compensate the staff."

BLAZING A TRAIL

Trotter says he didn't hesitate to break with restaurant industry tradition after asking himself, "If I were a server, how would I want to be paid?" He doesn't benchmark his restaurant against restaurant industry norms "because I disagree with so much of what happens in the industry. We can really only measure this restaurant against ourselves. All we can do is look at our business and ask what it will take to make it the best."

Another key benefit to the guaranteed wage plan is that it helps level out the quality of service in the dining room. "In other restaurants, the servers will fight over the big-spender table," says Trotter, whose restaurant attracts its share of high rollers. But the table with a single diner whose bill comes to $200 will get essentially the same level of service as a party of four that orders a $5,000 bottle of wine. Bounty-hunting waiters at tip-based restaurants would pamper the four-top (i.e., four-person table) at the expense of the single-diner table.

The compensation plan also fosters better relations between the front-of-the-house staff and the kitchen staff. One server recalls working at a restaurant where the waiters would routinely step back into the kitchen to tally their fistful of cash in full view of the chefs and dishwashers. The display of cash did not sit well with the kitchen staff, who grew to resent the prima donnas working the front of the house. So much for a sense of team spirit.

CALLING THE SHOTS

Unlike some restaurants that have developed server compensation plans that are less dependent on the capriciousness of tips, Charlie Trotter's does not fund its plan through a service charge on the customer's bill. Some restaurants have implemented a mandatory 18 percent service charge to pay their servers a regular wage. However, customers balked at being forced to pay the fee. They reported that they wanted to retain the discretion to tip their servers based on the quality of service they received. In essence, they wanted to be the boss. Some restaurateurs also were concerned that their servers who were no longer motivated to provide outstanding service in hopes of receiving a generous tip would require closer supervision.

Under the Trotter plan, the service staff is paid a minimum rate of $3.09 per hour. The restaurant then finances the balance through a pool of customer tips enough to equal the guaranteed fixed income of the server. Carle explains that the $3.09 figure is 40 percent less than the minimum wage, which the state allows when there is a pooled compensation arrangement. "The amount is really superfluous. It comes to $124 a week," she says. "The bulk of their compensation comes from the amount that is guaranteed from the pool of tips."

THE BONUS ROUND

The potential flaw in the system is that there might be a deficit in tips. If there is an annual deficit, however, Charlie Trotter's will make up the difference, although that has yet to happen. In the event that there is a substantial surplus in the pool, the money is paid out to the servers as a bonus.

The average per-person check at Trotter's is about $150 without tax or tip. With the average tip running about 18 to 20 percent, the tip for a table of two is about $55 to $60. Servers at the restaurant handle an average of six tables a night, most of them two-tops (that is, two guests at one table). Compensation under the system adopted in 1997 is comparable to what servers made under the old system. The big difference is that the pay is regular.

The restaurant consulted with its lawyers and accountants over the legality of pooling tips, which is illegal in some states. In Illinois, however, money collected as tips can be paid out as compensation. It's similar to the traditional system where the house tips 20 percent to a bartender or service assistant. Trotter's took it one step further by extending the pool to servers.

"Our plan is in the best interest of the guest and the people who work here," says Trotter. "It allows us to further achieve excellence through longer-term relationships with our employees. The plan is not based on what the industry standard is for service or food or ambiance."

A BLIND FAITH IN HIS STAFF

Trotter endows his well-paid, highly motivated service staff with the right to make their own judgment calls in the heat of battle. "All the rules that I articulate must be specifically followed—unless you need to break them." Yet there isn't the least bit of confusion among the service staff about what he means.

The front-of-the-house team implicitly understands that doing whatever it takes to delight a guest—even if it requires bending a few rules—goes to the heart of Trotter's value-added "there's no such word as no" service philosophy.

One of the bedrock rules at Charlie Trotter's is that there should always be a service staff member—a server, a server assistant, a food runner, or a sommelier—in each of the dining rooms. When a guest has a request or simply looks up from the table, his or her glance should be met with a response. A guest should never have to raise or wave a hand or call out for assistance.

THE POWER OF EMPOWERMENT

"I want the service staff to feel that they're empowered to make their own decisions. Nobody is looking over their shoulder saying: 'Why did you have to spend an extra $54 on that table by throwing in an extra bottle of wine and a cookbook.' The message is that we have enough confidence in your judgment to contribute to the overall experience of the guest."

While strict guidelines underlie the service, there is enormous latitude for an infectious spontaneity, flexibility, and common-sense resourcefulness on the part of the service team. As inventor Thomas Edison once put it: "Hell, there are no rules here. We're trying to accomplish something."

And so is Charlie Trotter. "You have to adopt a blind faith that not everything can be measured. Corporate America is reluctant to take a leap of faith unless the return on investment can be quantified. But I'm convinced that if you take care of the top line, the bottom line will take care of itself."

Trotter says he's not preoccupied with the restaurant's bottom line. "If I were, I wouldn't be willing to give away $3,000 or more a week in wine or cookbooks or extra courses. That's more than $150,000 a year that I regard as money well spent to push things over the edge."

But Trotter is not giving away the store. "I certainly monitor things. The servers have to ring in any value-added food or wine. I have a document of that each day. Sometimes I'll ask a server why he or she opened another bottle of wine, and usually a simple explanation is good enough. They don't have to come and justify their decision on the spot. They are empowered to make that call in the moment because they are on the floor dealing with the guests. What it says to the staff is 'I completely trust you. Do it. I'm sure you have your reasons.'"

There have been times when a server waived the charge or "comped" an entire meal if the server believed that things didn't go well for the guest. At a table for two, that could mean a $350 to $500 loss for the restaurant. "Maybe that was extravagant, but it's not the end of the world," says Trotter. "I think it's stimulating for the server to be able to give something extra to a guest—a foie gras course and wine to go with it, for example. At many restaurants a server can't even provide an after-dinner drink to a guest without the manager's permission. The price of empowerment is cheap because it's really investing back into our patrons. The net effect is that this restaurant is booked for three months out."

"Charlie Trotter's gives the servers the tools we need to make a guest's experience the best it can be. A couple made reservations with us several months in advance but later realized it coincided with their daughter's birthday. They didn't want to disappoint her so they called to ask if they could bring her along. We made the little girl feel comfortable by giving her a quick tour of the kitchen, where the pastry chefs let her taste some of the chocolate they were preparing. Everyone was happy. Service is the execution of the restaurant's vision. It's putting the ball in the hoop, as Charlie likes to say."

Jerry Slater, server

STOPPING AT NOTHING

Trotter's service staff appreciate his trust in them, particularly those who worked in environments where every nickel had to be justified. Jason Platt was a server in the restaurant of a four-star hotel for several years before he joined Charlie Trotter's. "I did not have the discretion to do anything extra for a guest. Everything had to go through channels."

At Charlie Trotter's, however, Platt has the power to add a course or subtract a charge from the bill. For example, Platt has added cheese courses or a flight of dessert wines for guests if he believed it would help accent their evening. And there have been times when he removed an item or items from a bill, like the time a progression of wines wasn't perfectly synchronized with the delivery of the courses. "Gestures like that can help you turn a table in the right direction," says Platt. "Maybe there was a delay at the front door that started the evening off on the wrong foot."

Kurt Sorensen says Trotter "is very good about more or less allowing us to do what we want to do. For example, we can go back into the kitchen and say: 'Let's organize an extra course for this table.' Or I can say to the kitchen that the guests at a table are getting quite full, why don't we cut a course."

Another employee echoes Sorensen's sentiment. "We can do almost anything here. We have all sorts of value-added tools that cost us little in the way of money and little in the way of time. For example, giving a six-minute tour is not going to make a great deal of difference to a service staff member, but it could make the difference between a really good dining experience and a really great dining experience for a guest. In some cases, less is more. It's not always necessary to do an extra course or an extra glass of wine."

COOL STUFF FOR THE CUSTOMER

Sommelier Belinda Chang says that having such a wealth of options with which to enhance the guest's evening is one of the benefits of her job. "It's great to be in a position to tell the guests that they are not restricted in any way. There's all this cool stuff that you don't know about, but that I'd be happy to tell you about."

Diners seem to appreciate the flexibility that Charlie Trotter's service team can bring to the table. A Florida physician wrote Trotter praising the service provided by Chang and contrasted her style with that of the service team at another respected Chicago restaurant. "In contrast to Ms. Chang, however, the servers were stiff, formal, and generally unwilling to make the changes that we requested. We did persist and the changes were made. Ms. Chang insisted from the start that flexibility was the rule of the house. Her buoyant good spirits, knowledge, and attention to detail greatly enhanced our dining experience."

Chang tells her guests that there's more than meets the eye at Charlie Trotter's. Behind the scenes, a team of nearly twenty top-flight chefs are working with some of the greatest foodstuffs in the world. "I tell them: 'We can do whatever you want.' I am happy to help them customize their courses. For example, with the vegetable menu, I make it clear that seafood could be added to that degustation menu because it still fits into that lighter profile."

Guests who find neither the vegetable nor the grand menu to their liking can choose à la carte style from a list of alternative dishes. Chang's bent for customization when she was a server put a strain on the kitchen, but she believes the extra effort on her part as well as on the kitchen's "makes the guests feel more appreciated."

TAKING IT TO THE LIMIT

And Charlie Trotter certainly won't fault Chang for putting the kitchen and the front of the house through some extra hoops to delight a guest. "I don't think guests truly appreciate how flexible we are. They don't realize how much farther they could have gone with a meal or a wine progression. The idea is that there is no such word as *no* here. I firmly believe that if guests trust us, we can blow their mind. But we have to win their trust."

While Trotter's service staff and kitchen staff are willing to bend over backward, he says it's important not to confuse the restaurant's "no such word as no" service concept with the notion that the customer is always right. Some guests can make unreasonable demands. "We're certainly not going to tell them that they're wrong; we're not going to argue with them. We'll do our best, but they may not be the kind of customer we want to serve again. But while they are here, we'll take the high road and keep it positive."

For guests worth keeping, Trotter says he and his staff will lavish them with inspired dishes accompanied by great wines served by a staff that's adopted his customer-is-king mindset. "It's more about learning a philosophy than a set of rules. If you understand the big picture, you can apply it across the board here."

SERVICE POINTS

To build and maintain an empowered, motivated service staff keep these service points in mind:

- Lead; don't manage.

- Inspire; don't motivate.

- Show your staff that no job is too insignificant by pitching in yourself on some of the little things.

- Convince young employees that hard work early in their career is essential to long-term success. Teach them the value of an apprenticeship in their chosen profession.

- Get tough with employees who are performing at a substandard level.

- Inspire employees with works of beauty. Bring them to events where they can appreciate the well-turned-out efforts of others.

- Let criticism from a supervisor, a guest, or a coworker motivate employees to perform at their best.

- Watch for employees whose performance plateaus after conquering initial challenges. Inspire them to exert themselves anew.

- Create a nontraditional compensation plan to better retain employees.

- Benchmark your business against your own goals, not against industry standards that may be less stringent than your own.

- Lay down the law, but grant employees the discretion to break the rules under appropriate circumstances.

- Create a system that allows you to monitor giveaways and other value-added calls your employees make.

- The customer isn't always right. Some of them aren't worth keeping, especially those who don't appreciate what your business is trying to do.

- Encourage spontaneity, flexibility, and common-sense resourcefulness among your staff.

5

Learning the Ropes on a Tight Ship

Service staffers at Charlie Trotter's who may be looking for guidance won't find it in an employee manual because there is none. Charlie Trotter finds manuals too restraining. New employees learn their steps through a combination of role playing, observing, and being carefully mentored by a more senior employee. One thing service employees quickly learn is that they're operating on a very fast track.

Jerry Slater, a recently hired server with a look as innocent as the boy next door, was facing some tough customers.

One woman simply couldn't comprehend the multicourse tasting menus at Charlie Trotter's. "I don't get it," she said as she puzzled over the grand and vegetable menus that Slater had just handed her.

A man at the four-person table wasted no time in announcing that he'd never been to a restaurant like Charlie Trotter's before as he slapped down the menu and asked for a steak. "I'm kind of a steak guy. I'd like it with every course." Slater politely explained that the restaurant doesn't serve steak, but as an alternative, the kitchen could include beef tenderloin with one or some of the evening's savory courses. Apparently satisfied with the response, man the asked about the beer selection.

"What kind do you have?" Slater, who previously had been the dining room manager of a well-regarded restaurant in Northwest Indiana, explained that Trotter's carries two premium beers—Goose Island from Chicago and Anchor Steam from San Francisco. Although he seemed disappointed at the depth of the beer selection, the man ordered a Goose Island.

WHAT? NO COCKTAILS?

The other woman at the table said she would like a cocktail. "I'm sorry, but we don't serve distilled beverages," Slater told her. He suggested a glass of champagne as an alternative. Looking miffed, the woman nevertheless acceded to his champagne suggestion.

When Slater returned from the bar area with the drinks, he answered additional questions about both the savory course and the dessert menus. "We offer more than just the two desserts listed on the menu. We have several alternates," Slater told a guest who sounded unhappy about the two offerings on the dessert menu. He explained that the kitchen would be happy to customize any part of the menus.

From across the room, Jason Platt, a server known for his quick wit and lively sense of humor, broke the ice. "I've never seen such a difficult table in the year that I've been here." The room erupted in laughter at Platt's observation during one of the restaurant's Wednesday afternoon tough-love role-playing sessions. The guests at the table were actually four of Slater's fellow service staff members— Debra Torres, Rene Roman, Belinda Chang, and Ari Kastrati.

Senior server Paul Larson, who was supervising the exercise, called for order in the first floor dining room as he prepared to weigh in on Slater's performance. "The greeting was warm and the drink order was handled promptly. He was very flexible as he offered a number of alternate dishes. The dessert philosophy was well articulated. Questions about the menu were well handled," said Larson. But he saw room for improvement. "We do serve some distilled beverages such as cognac and single-malt scotch, and we do have aperitifs," he said.

LADIES FIRST

Larson was critical of the way Slater delivered the drinks to the table. He reached over a guest instead of going around him. Larson also noted that a little chivalry was in order. Serve the women before serving the men, he suggested.

Larson opened the floor to critiques of Slater's role playing. Torres said that based on the uncertainty over the menu expressed by some of the guests, Slater could have pointed out that the menus can be abandoned entirely. He could have offered to simply let Charlie Trotter cook for them, meaning the kitchen would completely customize a series of dishes. Another server said Slater could have suggested the table order a bottle of wine as they were all over the board on their drink requests.

Larson then marched the service staff through a variety of nettlesome situations that can and will crop up on the floor on any given evening. The scenarios ranged from guests who are arguing with each other at the table to guests who are only on their second course but suddenly realize that they have to be at the theater in thirty minutes. At the end of the session, Larson walked over to Slater and gave him a sheet of his written comments. He also threw in a word of encouragement.

Slater had survived his trial by fire and was ready for just about anything on the floor in the weeks and months ahead. Role-playing training exercises are more complicated than instructional videos or manuals, but they more effectively teach the service employee to make a decision in the moment, which is especially important at Trotter's, where spontaneity and self-reliance are highly valued.

WE DON'T NEED NO STINKIN' MANUAL

Nothing is drawn from a training manual, because there isn't one. Charlie Trotter doesn't do things by the book. "We don't want to be hindered by a training manual because we are so excited about the idea of spontaneity and flexibility. Manuals are pretty impersonal, and they tend to impose a rigid structure. It's all about what you can't do. Handing a new employee that kind of manual is not a very encouraging way to begin a relationship with a company."

Because the restaurant does not have multiple shifts or multiple units, "It's still fairly simple for me and the managers to impart the way we do things here. We can make adjustments along the way. But if this was a larger operation, it might be necessary to put everything in writing, to codify it more."

While Trotter doesn't have ten service commandments etched in stone, he half-kiddingly estimates that there are some ten thousand unwritten service points that staffers will come to know.

An important point to remember is not to get too comfortable with your role, because you may be playing another one at any given moment, says Trotter. "If you can tend bar or act as a maitre d' or wait on a table, you are more valuable to me and to the guest. And the more things you can do around here, the more interesting your day becomes. The employee finds that invigorating."

"Trotter's service staff is among the best trained I've ever encountered. His wine list has depth in every category. The amenities are all first class."

Esquire

GET IT RIGHT

A service staffer will spend his or her early months on the job working in the shadow of a manager or a more experienced server. Mitchell Schmieding explained how he helped indoctrinate a recent hire:

"I shadowed everything that he did. He was sometimes addressing people as 'folks.' We say 'ladies and gentlemen.' I told him he handled a table's wine order well, except that he placed the wine glasses in the wrong position. I reminded him that after you clear a table, the next step is to put down the flatware. He told me he wanted to first pour them wine, but I explained that the next thing that's going to happen is that the food is going to arrive. If the food goes on the table before the flatware does, you've committed an error."

Schmieding also corrected the new server's habit of touching the back of guests' chairs when he would address them. He also admonished the new server, who like Schmieding is over 6 feet tall, for bending like a willow tree in a brisk wind to talk to the guests. Servers should stand upright and keep their hands off tables and chairs when talking to guests. He says those are some of the standards and practices that are conveyed to the new employee in person rather than through a manual.

The length of the shadowing process depends on how quickly the new service employee acquires the required skills and adopts Trotter's value-added mindset. Some employees are ready to leave the nest after only two months, others may take as long as a year, says Schmieding.

Paul Larson says new hires are often assigned to assist a more senior server at the restaurant's famed kitchen table. For veteran servers, the assignment is a coveted one. But for the newly hired, the assignment can be a pressure cooker. Not only is table 86 the most sought-after table in the restaurant, it's a only a few steps from Charlie Trotter's expediting post, where he scrutinizes each dish before it is served. Trotter will often keep one eye on the new hire to make sure he or she is cut out for the job. "He's always encouraging and correcting the service people at that table, giving pointers and leading the way," says Larson.

KITCHEN PATROL

The new hire will also spend time in the kitchen, observing the flow, watching how the food is prepared, and tasting the food. "It's important for them to understand the dynamic of food as it heads off to the different dining rooms. The new server has to understand how the timing works. If the timing is off, it begins to break down."

Larson, the restaurant's most senior server, had many years of service before he joined Trotter's. But he says his skills were elevated by such mentors as Trotter, Schmieding, and Mark Signorio. "It was a matter of learning by example. I would watch carefully as they talked to or waited on a table. They might say something a certain way. I would adapt my style to the way they did things." The level of teamwork at Trotter's impressed him. "We are constantly pouring wine at a table for each other or describing dishes for each other if we are otherwise occupied."

A training manual could not possibly instruct a new staffer on this level of service, says Larson. "You can learn so much here by just watching and listening. That's how I learned."

He learned the gospel of value-added service from Charlie Trotter, who, he says, instills it in the service staff. "It's that part of service where you're not necessarily asked to do something, but you anticipate what's needed at the table and carry it to another level. For example, if out-of-town guests ask you to recommend another restaurant they could visit while they are here, I wouldn't just give them a recommendation, but I would make the reservation for them. You couldn't possibly learn that way of thinking from a book."

COMBINING KNOWLEDGE WITH PASSION

A "never say no" attitude combined with a deep understanding of the food and wine that are being served are what sets servers at Trotter's apart from other restaurants, says Kevin Cronin. "I believe some of the servers here have better food and wine knowledge than a lot of cooks at other restaurants." Servers and sommeliers routinely taste each bottle of wine that is opened to assure that it is true to taste. Their palates are refined through wine tastings that are often incorporated into the Wednesday afternoon training sessions.

Each server owns a copy of the *New Sotheby's Wine Encyclopedia* by Tom Stevens. Servers are regularly tested on their knowledge of that book. During one session, for example, servers were given a two-page test to measure their knowledge of wine from Burgundy. The test included such questions as: "Explain 'Monopole' and give two examples from our wine list." "Name the classic food match for Chablis." "Where is St. Aubin and when would you recommend it?" Questions are designed to prepare the servers for the kinds of questions they may face on the floor. Servers are also trained to recognize when a wine clashes with the food being served at the table. If that were the case, a sommelier and the kitchen would be immediately notified to begin making adjustments.

MAPPING A PLAN

In addition to the Wednesday training sessions, the staff gather late each afternoon for about thirty minutes with Trotter to prepare for the evening ahead. At one particular preservice meeting, the service staff had their ties and their game faces firmly in place. The well-coifed, dark-suited wait staff huddled around a marble-topped island counter in the studio kitchen to await Charlie Trotter.

In a dress shirt and suit jacket, Trotter strode solemnly into the room to begin the meeting. It's an opportunity, he says, to get every member of the service team on the same page before the guests begin filing in. His presence at the thirty-minute meetings underscores how seriously the chef-owner takes his front-of-the house staff. Without the meeting, execution during service would not be nearly as crisp, which is why he attends and presides at three-quarters of them. Managers run the meeting in his absence.

Trotter scanned the room as if counting noses and asked whether everyone was there. "How about the kitchen?" he inquired. Chef de cuisine Matt Merges, standing in a doorway at the back of the room, thrust up his hand to announce his presence. "Who's at the front door?" asked Trotter, making sure an early arriving guest would be greeted with a human presence.

Check and double-check.

Pacing pensively, Trotter told the twenty-two-member service team that he hoped everyone's new year was off to a good start. He apologized to them for missing the last few nights. He explained that he his wife, Lynn, and their son, Dylan, spent a long weekend out of town to celebrate the couple's tenth wedding anniversary.

MIDCOURSE CORRECTIONS

He then began calling on his service team members to learn about any recent developments. Paul Larson spoke first. "A table was talking to your mom (Dona-Lee Trotter, who provides restaurant tours on weekends) about how they've been unable to get a Guest-Chef-for-a-Day certificate. They've been to several charity events where they were auctioned off, but they've been unsuccessful." Trotter responded by saying that winning the coveted certificates at charity auctions or raffles isn't the only way to earn the opportunity to spend an evening in chef whites with Trotter and his kitchen staff. A certificate could be secured with a $500 minimum donation to Charlie Trotter's Culinary Education Foundation. "We need to let people know that," he said.

Trotter turned to Christian Giles. "Any comments tonight, Christian?" "Yes. If you see things that need to be repaired, call it to someone's attention. Let a manager know. Don't just assume it will get fixed on its own." Point well taken, said Trotter, who is fastidious about maintaining the restaurant's top-of-the-line equipment.

Holding the floor, Giles offered another suggestion. "I've been over to the store (Trotter's To Go), and it looks amazing. The product is wonderful," he said. "But what's missing is a menu from here, perhaps the previous night's menu." He said a guest who might have been particularly fond of a dish could buy something similar at the store. "That's a great idea. Let's do that. In fact, we need to talk up the store to our guests. The reservationists are now mentioning the store when people call," said Trotter.

PIZZA, PIZZA

Jason Platt weighed in with what he called a "How come" question of Trotter. "We have these really great sandwiches at the store. Why don't we have any gourmet pizzas?" Trotter replied that gourmet pizzas may be added to the mix. "We're taking it one thing at a time. Let's see how it goes in the next couple of months."

He called on sommelier Belinda Chang for an update. "Our Bordeaux selections will double in the next couple of weeks. There's so much cool stuff coming," she said and recited a list of coming attractions as waiters reached for pens to record their names.

"The staff are very flexible as they measure the tone of each diner in the restaurant. There is nothing scripted about them. While they have the technical aspects down, they also manage to be very spontaneous. It's more than just putting the forks in the right place on the table."

Charles Sitzes, a Chicagoan who has been dining at the restaurant since its earliest days

"Anyone else?" asked Trotter. He then announced some good news and some bad news. The bad news first. "After thirteen and a half years of charging you $1 for the staff meal, we will need to start charging $2 for the meal starting tomorrow. Food is getting more expensive." There were no signs of a mutiny.

WE'VE GOT YOU COVERED

The good news was that staff members who were paying a small portion of their health care premium would no longer have to pay anything out of pocket. "Last year, as you know, the amount that the restaurant was paying for health insurance shot through the roof, but the prices have now fallen. So we will be paying for the entirety of your health coverage." He reminded the staff that those who have been there for at least three months but less than one year qualify for 50 percent coverage. "So there's some incentive for you new people to stay with us for a while and qualify for 100 percent coverage," he said.

His last piece of business that evening was to seek volunteers to help with a charity event at the end of the year, the Harvest of Hope dinner at Chicago's Four Seasons Hotel. "We will partner with Sara Lee Corporation, and our goal is to raise $1 million for the Mercy Home for Boys and Girls and for the Joffrey Ballet. The event will consist of a reception, an auction, and a dinner. I need a couple of you to help write letters and to recruit auction items. If you're interested, please let me know."

Trotter returned to his office to collect his chef's jacket and report for duty in the kitchen that evening. As he swept past the glass-walled studio kitchen wine cellar, he conducted a quick inspection of the large-format bottles.

THE CALM BEFORE THE STORM

After Trotter's departure, the staff turned its attention to the night ahead. Merges described a last-minute change on a dish from the grand menu. "Is the caviar Russian?" inquired a server. "Yes," he replied. Servers described several dishes on the alternate list, foodstuffs that don't appear on the regular menu. The alternate dishes that night included fluke fish, squab, quail, venison, lamb, and bison.

Chang read off a list of wines that were not available that night because the last bottles had been drawn from the cellars. Dining room manager Dan Fitzgerald alerted the staff to guests at tables who had food allergies. There was a party coming on a gift certificate, and a time was established for the arrival of the kitchen table party.

Fitzgerald also alerted the staff to some special guests that were planning to visit the restaurant that evening. Alerts are routinely issued for celebrities, regular customers making a return visit, or people from the culinary field such as chefs and sommeliers. "Offer to cook for the party at table 34."

Members of the kitchen staff, such as Merges or a sous chef, are always in attendance to describe a new dish or other changes in a menu. To enhance their own food knowledge, several servers each night are called upon to describe a particular dish on the menu. Fitzgerald had the last word at the meeting. "We begin seating in the dining room in four minutes," he said as the service team sprung to its positions.

MEETINGS WITH A PURPOSE

"We meet for different reasons," says Trotter. "Some meetings are designed to instruct, some are to inspire, and others are designed to reiterate certain service points." Variety is important. Otherwise meetings become routine. Comments, either good or bad, on a customer satisfaction survey are sometimes the subject of a preservice meeting. "A letter might make the point that the delivery of the food seemed poorly timed, or that the room suddenly grew to be very cold, or that guests at a nearby table weren't properly dressed, or that a guest felt that a dessert was a bizarre combination of flavors," says Trotter. "That kind of information is valuable to share with the team. We have to know those things if we hope to improve."

Trotter says by publicly airing a problem raised in a letter, the staff can make an adjustment. Suggestions, which would otherwise go unspoken, begin to flow. Conversely, if a letter applauds an action by a service staff member, "We can endorse it and reinforce it as the way things should be done."

Trotter will sometimes begin the meeting by asking the staff for a candid assessment of the previous night's performance. There's often a range of postmortem reports—from mistakenly serving a grand menu dish to a guest who ordered a vegetable menu to more positive observations: "The energy in the dining room was terrific" and "The guests at table 21 were really psyched." Everyone is entitled to have their say at the meetings, says Trotter. But it's not the place for long-winded speeches because the meetings never last more than thirty minutes. Chop-chop, as they say in the trade.

The service team gathers informally each afternoon prior to the preservice meeting to share a meal. In the room where they collect hangs a framed quote from Winston Churchill that reads: "To improve is to change. To be perfect is to change often."

Although Charlie Trotter allows that perfection is probably impossible, change is not. He changes menus nightly, the wine list is ever evolving, and he loves to switch the roles that his service staff play. Change is good, especially when it's done in the quixotic pursuit of perfection.

"You have to keep people challenged. They don't want to do the same things over and over again. They get bored. Secondly, it's fun for people to be a little scared, to do something they've never done before. It's a chance for them to reinvent themselves," says Trotter.

KEEPING THINGS ON EDGE

To keep people on their toes, Trotter will frequently change dining room assignments even if a team of two servers, a server assistant, and a sommelier have their steps down to a well-honed routine. The moment something becomes routine is the moment that things begin to slip, he believes. It's when people start going through the motions. The passion and the intensity that are essential to blowing the guests' minds begin to wane.

But Trotter will never allow an employee to just fax it in. He's quick to recognize when an employee has reached a plateau and seems to lack the drive to climb higher. He has no problem creating a sense of anxiety or nervousness among his staff.

"If anxiety means eager and unsure, then I'm all for that because the staff person is more alert, more in the moment. They are less apt to go on autopilot. It's like getting well-dressed to go out. It creates a little bit of nervousness," says Trotter. "I don't set out to create tension or anxiety, but I'm willing to let anxiety or tension happen because it creates a higher level of concentration."

THE VIRTUE OF VERSATILITY

Trotter does more than tweak dining room assignments every few weeks to keep the juices flowing. He wants his front-of-the-house staff to be jacks-of-all-trades. A server assistant should be able to pour wine, a receptionist should be able to run food or present a menu, and a server should be able to tend bar. Servers need to be able to properly maintain a station's silverware, tablecloths, and stemware—a key responsibility of a server assistant.

Chefs are sometimes called upon to play front-of-the house roles. They visit tables in the dining room to describe a dish, and they occasionally take guests on tours of the restaurant. They need to be every bit as articulate on their feet as their front-of-the-house counterparts. The ad hoc front-of-the-house assignments make the chefs more empathetic for the servers who face the customers each night. "You're more valuable to me and the guest when you can wear several hats," Trotter says. "The more a staff person is exposed to, the more invigorated that employee will be."

"When the plates are brought to the table there is always someone available to describe the dish and make sure everyone understands what they have in front of them. They are sensitive to the conversations going on at the table and always wait for the right moment. The staff are just as efficient and flawless at clearing a table, doing it in a way that minimizes interfering with the guests."

Jim Gaby, Washington, D.C.–based software consultant and longtime customer

Employees often ask Trotter for permission to try on a new role—if even for a week or two. Matt Merges runs one of the best kitchens in America. But for a week in the fall of 2000, he swapped his toque and white chef's jacket for a conservative navy blue suit and waited tables. He also plans to spend a week as a valet, a week as a food runner, and a week as a glass polisher. He said he would execute each job with the same intensity as if he were preparing an eight-course meal. Merges says his week on the floor gave him valuable insights into the tastes and preferences of the diners—people he would otherwise never see, but who ultimately pay his salary.

No employee at the restaurant can claim that a particular job is "not my department" because Trotter believes there is no limit to what an employee's job is and what it can be. He also likes to blur the lines between departments and between individual responsibilities. Employees who want a firm job description won't get one from Trotter, who says that's unsettling for some people but energizing for others. "There's no formal employment structure. It's really more customized to the individual's capabilities."

TEAR DOWN THE WALLS

Trotter, who has worked both ends of the house, has broken down barriers, which has reduced traditional animosity between the kitchen and the front of the house. Take, for instance, the day when a semi loaded with Trotter's latest cookbook pulled up in front of the restaurant. The truck was quickly emptied by an impromptu team of chefs, servers, dishwashers, food runners, and the corporate office staff, who stacked the hundreds of books in the restaurant's garage.

A similar scene played out weeks earlier when a truck laden with large bags of flour pulled into the alley behind the restaurant. Employees from every corner of the restaurant materialized to form a bucket brigade to disgorge the truck's contents. No one was told to help empty the trucks. The employees did so naturally, reflecting the team spirit at Trotter's.

A TOUCH OF MAGIC

A big fan of basketball, Trotter notes how valuable a versatile player like Magic Johnson was to the Los Angeles Lakers when that team dominated the NBA in the late 1980s. In his rookie season, Johnson played point guard, power forward, and even center during the team's championship run.

Trotter says the risk that an employee cast into an unfamiliar role will make a serious mistake on the floor is slight. He loves to push employees into water that's over their head. But he says there's plenty of support for a service staffer who finds him- or herself floundering. "It will be a fairly controlled environment because you'll be working with a person more experienced in that role."

One staffer says Trotter will push an employee to discover his or her personal limit. "He'll try to push you over the edge sometimes, but you have to recover and come back."

While Trotter sees the learning of new roles as relatively risk-free, one employee feels the pressure. "The stakes are so high here, there's not a lot of time for hand-holding when someone is just hired or is in a new role. It's sink or swim," says the employee, who's managed to keep her ahead above water every time Trotter has pushed her into the deep end of the pool.

PUT ME IN COACH

Mitchell Schmieding says that cross training the service staff "creates an understanding, an empathy for each others' position and what it takes to do it. There is a respect for the job and the difficulties and preparation that come with it."

The cross training at Trotter's is done just like the training, through a process of observing, role playing, mentoring, and constant reinforcement of the restaurant's Olympian standards. New employees are assigned a shadow who will work in tandem with them with during a shift. "The coach is right there with you every step of the way," says Schmieding. An employee in cross training to wait on tables, for example, will be backstopped by a veteran server for at least a week.

Trotter also likes to keep employees challenged and on edge by casting them into completely different roles at the restaurant. For example, a server might be tapped for sommelier duty or a receptionist might be asked to wait tables. For some of his charges, he provides objectives with strict timetables and parameters. "I might say 'Call this person, do this by then, arrange for this, show me the product and then I'll sign off on it.'"

VARIETY'S THE SPICE OF LIFE

Sari Zernich is a good example of an employee who has handled a variety of roles. Zernich works in the corporate office, where her responsibilities include recipe testing for the Trotter cookbooks and coordinating many of restaurant's out-of-house events like book signings and charity auctions. Zernich, who has a degree in food science from the University of Illinois, began in the kitchen, but was tapped for more corporate assignments when she told Trotter that she was planning to take a job at Quaker Oats.

"For someone like Sari, I might tell her that I want a new bag for the restaurant that we could use for gifts. The only thing I would tell her was that I want the logo and the web site address on it. I would leave the design, the fabric, the color, and other considerations up to her. She would come back at some point with three different designs and explain her choices. She's been challenged to do something that she's never done before. It demonstrates the faith and trust I have in an employee."

Zernich's corporate office mate, Judi Carle, is the restaurant's accountant. Trotter asked Carle to apply her accountant's eye for detail to the series of cookbooks he began writing in the 1990s. In addition to balancing the books, Carle is also editing the books, the cookbooks, that is.

"Going the extra distance is a priority of Mr. Trotter's. The china is not restaurant china but the more delicate 'home' china that breaks more easily but looks prettier. Mr. Trotter's work station is covered with white linen so he can see whether a plate will leave a ring on the tablecloth or not. Regular customers never get the same meal twice since Mr. Trotter makes it a point to never repeat a dish. And every day, Mr. Trotter meets with the service staff to review the previous night's performance and to anticipate the needs of the coming evening. The waiters dress in business suits, à la the Secret Service minus the earpieces."

The New York Times

Mark Signorio, who began as a server, handles a variety of assignments under his loosely defined role as director of special projects and business development. Reached on his cell phone one morning, Signorio explained that he was busy stocking shelves at Trotter's To Go. "I'm the stock boy today," said the graduate of the prestigious Art Institute of Chicago. He has put his design degree to good use by lending his touch to the dining room and the restaurant's exterior design. He brings some of Trotter's visions to life at his home, where he prefers to spend most of his workweek. And on nights when an extra server is needed, Signorio suits up.

LEARNING THE ROPES ON A TIGHT SHIP

SERVICE POINTS

To bring new service staffers up to speed in an environment that operates without an employee manual, consider these service points:

- Teach employees valuable lessons about service with role-playing exercises. Have employees critique each other's performance and give each employee a written critique of his or her performance.

- Forget the training manual. Teach by example.

- Assign a "shadow" to mentor a new employee.

- Get all members of a service team on the same page with regular staff meetings.

- Have a top executive regularly attend meetings to send a message to the staff that they are important.

- Read customer letters—both positive and negative—at staff meetings. Use the sessions to assess the team's previous performance.

- Let everyone have a say at the meeting, but keep it short. Meetings at Trotter's never exceed thirty minutes.

- Once an employee has mastered a routine, it's time to change it. Keep the work force challenged and invigorated with cross training.

- Promote team spirit by blurring the lines between departments and individual responsibilities. Cross training employees creates a stronger sense of empathy and respect for another person's position.

PART III

EXECUTING: MAKING

GREAT SERVICE HAPPEN

EVERY DAY

No business is flawless. But Charlie Trotter's believes it can consistently approach that standard on the strength of its ability to read a customer, the various fail-safes that undergird its service, and its ability to intuitively and methodically gauge customer satisfaction. If an aspect of service falls, the organization is nimble enough to make the correction.

6

Building a One-on-One Customer Relationship

Successful businesses cultivate a sense of loyalty among their customers. It's cheaper than continuously prospecting for new ones. Charlie Trotter's keeps customers coming back for the sumptuous cuisine, but also because of the individualized treatment they receive at the hands of the service staff.

It's no accident that servers at Charlie Trotter's have a strong sense of ownership for each of their tables. It's by design.

At restaurants with formal servers, a maitre d' or captain will typically seat the guests and describe the menu. A front waiter will take the order, and a back waiter will serve the food. "It's confusing for the guests. They can't tell who's who," says Mitchell Schmieding.

At Trotter's, servers focus all of their energies on the three or four tables in their station. "The server does not run off to another room to do something else," says Schmieding. "He or she stays in the dining room and takes care of just about everything at that table. The server establishes a relationship with the guest. They will be together over the course of the next three hours. That works much better than having different people flash in for an order, never to be seen again."

Because servers at Trotter's work so closely with the guests, they become much more intuitive about their customers' likes and dislikes, unlike restaurants that shuttle through a stream of waiters and busboys. Servers at Trotter's anticipate what the guest will want rather than simply react to a series of requests. Because one person is responsible for everything that goes on at a table, little gets lost in translation. That's especially important when a guest has special food considerations such as a potentially harmful food allergy. In another restaurant a guest might indicate to a maitre d' that he is seriously allergic to onions, and that might get passed along to the next service person down the line that the guest simply doesn't like onions.

THE BUCK STOPS HERE

"Here the person taking the order is the same person who described it and the same person who will be placing it," says Schmieding. "That's not to say that we don't have teamwork, because we do. But there's an area of focus here. The server is the sole liaison between the restaurant and the guest."

Trotter's focus on customers is similar to the best hotels, such as the Ritz-Carlton, or the best retailers, like Nordstrom's, where a service employee personally takes ownership

"Trotter's servers are attentive without being overbearing. They don't hover at the table. I have never felt hurried through a dinner. But they always seem to be there at the right moment. In fact, they are there before you even thought about what you might need. They have a deep respect for the guests and they always give them the benefit of the doubt."

Dan Mjolsness, Chicago-based executive who has been a guest chef-for-the-day on three occasions

of a customer problem. It's up to him or her to resolve it to the customer's satisfaction. It is not the responsibility of the next person down the line.

At Trotter's, a service team includes a server assistant in each dining room, food runners, a sommelier, and a manager who moves in and out of the dining room and supports the server. Any one of those people can and will pitch in at a table, but the buck stops with the server. The server is the guests' primary point of contact and takes complete responsibility for their evening.

Belinda Chang says one of the best parts of her job is maintaining longstanding relationships with the restaurant's loyal customers. "Guests love it when they are recognized at the door," says Chang. For example, a couple wrote a glowing letter to Charlie Trotter about the gracious service she provided them one night. They reported in the letter that they were eager to make a return visit and expressed the hope that Chang would again be their server.

When the reservationist alerted Chang that the couple was returning, she made it a point to greet them at the restaurant's doorstep at 5:45 P.M. "I swooped them right through the door and took them directly to their table, where we discussed that evening's plan for food and wine. They didn't even have to think. They simply enjoyed a great dinner. We might ask guests like that if they'll allow us to forgo the formality of a menu and have the kitchen cook for them."

MAKE NEW FRIENDS, BUT KEEP THE OLD

Lavishing a little extra attention on a returning guest is not only rewarding on a personal basis, it's smart business. It's an axiom of marketing that it costs seven to ten times more to recruit a new customer than it does to retain an existing one. Therefore relationships are important at a business like Charlie Trotter's, which does not prospect for new customers. Trotter's does not advertise. Never has, never will. The restaurant puts guests in seats on the strength of its reputation.

When officials of Boeing Corporation celebrated their decision in May 2001 to relocate their headquarters from Seattle to Chicago, they did so at—where else—Trotter's. Media from around the world made mention or wrote stories about the dinner at the acclaimed restaurant.

Trotter says recognizing returning guests and their preferences is essential to any business. He stops by a neighborhood Starbucks three or four days a week on his way to the restaurant. Noticing that Trotter usually ordered the same kind of coffee on each visit, the clerk began making it the moment Trotter walked through the door. "This guy had been waiting on me for some time. He'd greet me with a smile when I walked in and would have my order for me. No questions asked," says Trotter, who notes that there is no shortage of coffee retailers in his neighborhood, but he's sold on the store that treats him like a friend.

CONNECTING WITH CUSTOMERS

It's that kind of connection, although on a grander scale, that Trotter wants his staff to make with loyal customers. "When guests return a third, fourth, or fifth time, do we treat them differently?" Trotter asks rhetorically. "Absolutely. Some would argue that all customers should be treated the same. But good and loyal customers should be treated differently. I'm not saying better, but differently. We know more about them."

He likens the care and feeding of regular customers at his restaurant to the way the better airlines treat their loyal customers. For example, they are given some preference when the aircraft is being boarded, upgrades on their service, and other forms of recognition. "There should be an incentive for being a regular customer," says Trotter. "For our regulars, we are trying to wrest the whole menu concept away from them. After guests have been with us a few times, we tell them: 'Forget the menu. Let us cook for you.' It's much more interesting doing it that way. By that stage of the relationship, we have discovered their likes and dislikes."

The more you know about a guest, the better, more customized service you can provide that guest, says Trotter, whose reservationist will store information about a returning guest in the restaurant's computerized database. The 1,500 people in the database receive mailings about special events at the restaurant. At Christmas, they receive a hand-signed card from Trotter.

A SERVER NEVER FORGETS

Trotter's veteran service staff have a strong collective memory. They will informally store away information about a dish or a wine that particularly pleased a guest on a previous visit. "It's a two-way street," says Trotter. "We're providing information about the dining experience to them, and they're providing information about their particular tastes to us. Sometimes the exchange of information takes place through direct questions; other times it's more subtle than that. It might be through observation."

Learning about a guest and building toward a fruitful, long-term relationship sometimes begins with the very first contact. "It could begin when they are making a reservation," says Trotter. "The guest might let it slip that it's his first visit to the restaurant. He is coming to celebrate his wife's fortieth

"Service at Charlie Trotter's means always putting the guests first. No matter what happens in the course of an evening, the guests are what are most important to us. Each person or each table is here for our benefit; without these guests, none of what we do would be worth the blood, sweat, and tears."

Christian Giles, server

109

birthday. We'll note that in the book and perhaps add an extra dessert that evening. He wasn't asking us to do that. It's just something we might do to begin what we hope is a long-lasting relationship."

Paul Larson, who has been with the restaurant more than ten years, is an invaluable asset because of his institutional memory. "He knows just about every friend of the restaurant, and they're delighted when they're recognized on a return visit," says a colleague. New hires, especially those working the front door, are schooled on the importance of recognizing a friend of the restaurant the moment he or she steps into the restaurant.

New hires are alerted at preservice meetings when a returning guest will be visiting the restaurant that evening. The service staffer might provide a brief description of the guest, or a more veteran staffer might tap the employee on the shoulder to remind him or her when a regular customer has arrived.

WELCOME BACK

"The last thing you want is for a loyal guest (such as one who's dined at the restaurant more than a hundred times!) to walk in and have the receptionist ask: 'What is the name on your reservation?'" says one front-of-the-house staffer. "Recognition is

> "As the restaurant has grown and changed over the years, the guest's expectation level is higher than ever before. We are always striving to improve our service technique. New ideas come up almost on a daily basis. I think the word 'refinement' is very important with regard to our personal style here at Charlie Trotter's. A warmer welcome or farewell to a guest is always possible. We have an intentional focus on downplaying pretensions. After every new award or accolade, we focus on humility and excellence."
>
> *Paul Larson, senior server*

a very key part of our service." The employee, who often greets guests at the front door, will go to great lengths to make the greeting as personal as possible.

Trotter does not want the front-door staff hovering over the reservation book. He wants them to have a strong sense of who's coming in that evening. Explains another front-door employee: "If you know you have a six-top coming in at 8 P.M., and they come in and announce themselves, you should not have to run back to the book to confirm. Rather, you take them directly to their table. You eliminate a stutter step. It's recognizing a guest without using the book. By essentially memorizing who's coming and when and where they are to sit, you're much more efficient at that first, critical moment."

If returning guests are properly recognized either through the reservation system or by a service staff member, the staff might do something extra for them. The server might give them an extra course, a gift bag with a cookbook or a dessert wine. The decision is the server's on the floor based on recognition of the guests. He or she does not have to go through a manager or Trotter, who gives employees the latitude do something special for guests like that.

Returning guests who have not alerted the reservationist that they were returning could go unrecognized, but it's not likely. A service staff member will inevitably recall the guest. For example, Belinda Chang one evening remembered a party of returning guests. She even recalled the kind of wine they had ordered and that they had been taken on a tour of the wine cellars and the kitchen. In cases like that, the staff will do something special to recognize them.

There's the temptation to go overboard for a returning guest, says one staffer. "Charlie reminds us that sometimes, less is more. It's not always necessary to throw on an extra course or bring them an extra glass of wine. It's often just a matter of saying, 'Hello. It's nice to see you again.'"

STRIKING THE RIGHT NOTE

Establishing a relationship with a new diner is more of a challenge
than renewing a relationship with a guest. Servers say they need to
carefully read the guest to determine the degree of interplay that's
appropriate at the table. "Some guests want to have a conversation
with you, but others do not," says Kurt Sorensen.

Trotter discourages servers from becoming overly familiar with
guests on their first visit, instead keeping the focus on the food,
wine, ambiance, and, of course, the service. "It's inappropriate for
servers to tell their life story or talk about what they did in college
or provide their home address to guests," says Trotter. "There are a
time and place for that, usually after a guest has been coming here
on a regular basis for a number of years. It's wonderful to get to that
stage with a guest. That's what it's all about."

TRUST ME

For the first-time diner and even some seasoned diners, the experience can be overwhelming. "It can be a case of information
overload," says Trotter. "We hand the guests a fifty-five-page wine
list and tell them about the two degustation menus. So it's a matter of building up their trust. The staff will explain that they can
pick out the wines or, if the guests are comfortable with it, we allow
them to make the choices. Sometimes it's a little bit of both." After
establishing a bond of trust, servers at Charlie Trotter's can more
capably manage the dining experience for their guests.

Server is actually the wrong term for the people who wait tables
at the restaurant, says Trotter. "They are really navigators or guides
for the evening. Their job is to understand and interpret as much as
they can at the table. The better the information they can exchange,
the better they can adjust to a particular circumstance, perhaps
adding a course or doing something special for the table."

PEELING THE ARTICHOKE

The savvy navigator/server is adept at asking a guest questions to gauge his or her needs for the evening. Simple "yes" or "no" responses generally aren't helpful. The servers will often press beyond the superficialities to get a stronger sense of what the guest thinks or wants. It's like peeling an artichoke. And you can't do it well unless you're a careful listener.

"Great service is about how you communicate to the guests and how the guests communicate to you," says Mark Signorio. "For example, if you are at a table and the guest is asking a lot of questions about how the fish is cooked or asks to have the fish cooked well, the guest may be telling you that he or she is a little squeamish about medium rare food. I might then ask the guest if he or she wants all of the meat or fish cooked all the way through."

"The servers have a sense for the right amount of conversation with a table. If a table wants to talk to the waiter or the sommelier, the staff will accommodate. Likewise, if a table prefers to sit and dine quietly, the staff will be sensitive to that. They properly gauge service for each table. They are always checking and monitoring all the tables to make sure everything is right."

Jim Gaby, Washington, D.C.–based software consultant and longtime customer

Then there are times when a guest will say nothing about a dish, but a discerning server will able to tell that he or she has some reservations about it. For example, says Signorio, the guest might only be eating the edges of the fish. "I'd go to the chef and tell him that the guest apparently prefers his fish cooked medium because he's not eating the rare fish. On the next course, I might have the chef leave off the clams and oysters. We would just tweak it a bit. Or I would serve it without telling them what I had done to the dish. People are very grateful for that. Sometimes they'll say, 'How did you know?'

"Charlie Trotter's is able to take our product and make magic out of it. It is rewarding to deliver the product to the restaurant's back door and see how enthusiastically it's accepted by the staff. Even though it's always an extremely busy time in Chef Trotter's high-performing kitchen, I have always been treated with great courtesy there. Making people comfortable is second nature to everyone there. You can't separate courtesy from service."

Janie Crawford, Crawford Farm, a lamb supplier for fine restaurants in Chicago and Madison, Wisconsin

and I'll say that I noticed you didn't touch the fish and my guess was that you don't like fish. So I eliminated your seafood course and brought you squab instead. They are really pleased by that."

Similarly, a guest might consistently request that cheese or some type of fat component be left out. "That would send a signal to me that the guest is trying to control what he or she is eating, perhaps because of a dietary restriction or a food allergy." With that kind of insight into the customer, the server has a better opportunity to make the dining experience more rewarding.

PLAYING A PROFESSIONAL ROLE

Sometimes a quick tutorial on a dish or its method of preparation can be helpful for a diner. "A guest might be asking, 'What's this?' or 'What's that?' This person is having a hard time understanding the menu, and overly technical explanations are only going to make matters worse.

"If, for example, a guest asks about duck confit, I could say that it's duck cooked in its own fat, but that's a very negative way of describing the dish," says Signorio. "Instead, I would say confit is an old-world way of preserving food products as the chef slowly braises the meat, allowing the fat and oil to rise to the top and seal in the flavor. The resulting flavors are intense, and the texture is extremely tender and moist. I might answer questions at several levels so the guest understands the premise. The goal is to make the guest more comfortable. It's not talking down to the guest at all."

It's sometimes more difficult to tease important information out of a guest who's dining on business as compared to a guest who's there for social purposes and in the company of a spouse or close friend. "It happens all the time with a business dinner. No one will say a word when asked about food allergies or other dietary restrictions. But later you will be pulled over by a guest who will sheepishly say that they don't like raw fish. But they would never say that when ordering in front of the people in their party."

WORK WITH ME

By contributing to the guest's comfort, even in a subtle way, the guest "will let you in a bit closer to let you create an enjoyable experience for that guest." By paying careful attention to a guest's response patterns, Signorio can get a better feel for how far he might be able to push the guest toward a dish he or she might be unfamiliar with or even uncomfortable with.

Signorio says it's important to get the guest to relax; otherwise the guest is on the defensive and the server will have little chance of leading the diner into uncharted culinary territory. The staff enjoys elevating the guests' palates—even those of the most seasoned diners. If the guest has bought into Signorio's persuasion, he'll resort to some light humor, saying: "'Now that wasn't so painful, was it?' You have to manage the guest's experience a little bit. There is some give and take. Once you find where the guest's comfort level is, you have a great opportunity to make a difference. There are also times when you need to know it's time to back off."

"SHOW THEM YOUR TEETH"

The guest's experience begins the moment he or she steps into the foyer-atrium, says Schmieding. "I can usually tell when someone coming in the front door is intimidated or uncomfortable. It could be because it's a first-time visit or because it's Charlie Trotter's. There is this huge expectation. Almost like meeting the Queen," he says with a chuckle. "It's as if the guest is saying, 'Am I going to genuflect properly? Is my palm sweaty? How do I address her?' It's one of those types of experiences for guests."

Schmieding says one of the simplest ways to disarm a guest is with a smile. "We impress the importance of smiling upon everyone. We tell them, 'Show them your teeth.' That often puts guests at ease immediately. If we have time with them in the foyer-atrium, we'll strike up a simple conversation. I might ask whether they've dined with us before. If the answer is no, I'll say, 'Oh, you're going to have a great time. Here's what you're going to experience. There are two different menus; both are fixed-price tasting menus.'"

Schmieding says it's critical that "We take care of the entire experience for the guest. To have the wrong dish for one guest will detract from the experience of the other guests."

The front-of-the-house staff have helped guide guests through some of the most delicate social situations—the first date. "When there is a lack of conversation or some level of discomfort, the staff know that we have to join in somehow and be a bit more entertaining, not in an insincere way, but just to keep the conversation going at the table," says Schmieding. "If people loosen up a bit they can enjoy the evening."

QUICK AND CONVERSANT ON THEIR FEET

Trotter wants his service staff to be agile enough to guide any guest in any situation toward an unforgettable evening. "One table might be there for the very first time and may not dine out much. The next table might be someone who is here once a month, and another table is someone who is here once or twice a year and also dines out in New York and Europe and Asia. They know every nuance. The same server must be able to provide a different level of experience for each guest at each table."

At the very least, says Trotter, it's important for the service staff to understand that guests are dining at the restaurant for a special reason and that they're willing to book a table months in advance and to dress more formally than they normally would. "They're investing a lot in the evening, and it's not just the money."

Servers who are sensitive to the guests' needs can help elevate the experience, says Trotter. No particular personality type does it better than the next. His staff has a broad range of personalities—from the hale fellow well-met type to the soft-spoken introvert.

Servers with more reserved styles occasionally prompt comments on the customer survey that they were distant or aloof, but Trotter believes some of that is a matter of misinterpretation. For some servers, humor is

"Charlie Trotter's is more than a place to dine. It is a serene and elegant temple to food and to wine. In the two-story atrium, wine racks reach from floor to ceiling. The mahogany wainscoting and the simple, classic furnishings are painstaking reproductions of Viennese architect Josef Hoffman's 1905 designs for the Café Fledermaus. All this to set off the culinary alchemy that is being worked in the kitchen. Trotter has been called a 'bold experimentalist' and an 'innovator,' and has won for his restaurant the highest acclaim. But most importantly, Charlie Trotter, the man, and Charlie Trotter's, the restaurant, have earned the undying love of many delighted diners."

Relais & Chateaux

"An even more stupendously delectable 12-course, three-hour extravaganza is served only at a single table inside the kitchen, priced at $150 per person. Running a kitchen this way is incomparably more complex than keeping up with even a very large à la carte menu. Each night's menus must be crafted afresh, and often re-created on the fly. You never know when someone is going to show up with a salsify allergy, or who had the roasted saddle of Scottish hare with red-wine emulsion, requiring a sudden substitution. The tasting menu is meant to dazzle. Trotter claims he's had one customer 265 times and he has never served him the same meal twice."

Newsweek

an important part of their repertoire. Others would never use it. Some know more about wine than others. Some have a powerful command of the cuisine and its ingredients. What they all have to be is good on their feet. "I'm constantly encouraging people to think about how they say things," says Trotter.

He's happy that his staff brings a variety of sensibilities to the table and can provide guidance in unique ways. "I think it's an advantage that we have such a diversity because we encounter so many different types of guest and types of situations each night."

SERVICE POINTS

To build stronger bonds with customers consider these service points:

- Create a single or primary point-of-contact system for your customer.

- Make it clear that employees should take responsibility for a customer and any problems that might arise, rather than assuming that another staffer will step in.

- Create a system that will allow you to recognize loyal customers.

- Recognition does not have to be elaborate. A simple "Hello. It's nice to see you again" will often do it.

- Make loyal customers feel special. Include them in mailings or provide them a value-added service. It's substantially less expensive to keep a customer than it is to recruit a new one.

- Listen carefully for cues from customers. That information could be valuable in establishing a long-term relationship.

- Have employees guide customers through what may appear to them as a maze of information.

- Employees should smile or strike up a conversation to put a customer at ease.

- Learn what the customer wants. Gently inquire until you get substantive information.

- Hire a diversity of people and personalities; this can help a business cope with a diversity of situations.

7

Back Stage at
Charlie Trotter's

There's more than meets the eye at Charlie Trotter's, where a well-honed communications system invisibly underpins the service on the floor and helps let the left hand know what the right hand is doing. Striking such synchronicity is critical to the success of any service-oriented business.

Each dish at Charlie Trotter's tastes best when it's served at the right moment, which requires the back of the house and the front of the house to work harmoniously. The forty-five kitchen staff and service team members need to be acutely aware of what's taking place in their respective domains to deliver a flawless dining experience. It's a delicate balance.

This is hardly unique to Trotter's or the restaurant business. Interdepartmental or interdivisional cooperation and communication are critical to the success of any enterprise. Within an advertising agency, for example, the creatives must work hand-in-glove with the account executives to develop a successful ad campaign for a client. Within a corporation, coordination between the marketing department and their counterparts in sales is absolutely essential to a new product's launch. Striking the yin-yang balance is never easy, especially at Trotter's, where the pace—at least behind the scenes—is breakneck and the probability of a disconnect between the front and back of the house is high.

"If the service team performs brilliantly, then the food is going to taste even better," says Trotter. "And the service will look even better if the food is cooked and delivered in a timely manner."

The two teams, staffed equally at about twenty-two members each, complement each other quite well, says Trotter. "We have an articulate, well-groomed service team that maintains extraordinary decorum while dealing with difficult circumstances on the floor. Not everyone can do that. And we have an amazing kitchen team that is highly disciplined and is capable of concentrating for long periods of time to create this amazing cuisine. The two teams need to understand that while they have their own areas of specialization, they are all part of the same unit."

THE BEST-LAID PLANS

There is much that can upset the balance at the restaurant on any given evening. A guest might leave the table, to visit the rest room or step outside to speak on a cell phone, moments before a dish is to arrive. Hold everything.

A guest might be eating at a slower-than-normal place. A table might switch directions on a wine progression, precipitating a change in the next several courses out of the kitchen. A guest might send a dish back to the kitchen complaining that it's not prepared to his or her liking. Guests might arrive forty minutes late. A guest might announce that he is allergic to a particular foodstuff or ingredient. There can be complications in the kitchen. A spill. A line that's not firing properly. A sudden deluge of orders. A blizzard or a thunderstorm can easily wreak havoc on an evening.

But if the kitchen understands the complications on the floor, and the service team understands the complications in the kitchen, it all should still work—and it almost always does. The kitchen, the restaurant's nerve center, essentially calls the shots, unlike most restaurants, where a server will march into the kitchen and tell the chefs to fire up an entrée.

But it's not quite that simple at Trotter's, where guests receive anywhere from seven to fifteen courses over the course of a three-hour dining experience. With 125 to 130 guests a night, that's a lot of plates of food, and that's why the restaurant has twenty cooks.

According to Trotter, "The food has to be meticulously timed. The chefs are cooking the food when they're ready to cook the food, and they're sending it out when they are ready to send it out. They're on a flow with the food. They're going to do this fire and this fire. They're going to cook this fish and this vegetable dish. They're going to do these meats or these birds. But for that to work, the kitchen must have a keen awareness as to the timing of any given table."

PEERING THROUGH THE PERISCOPE

Although there is a window on the door between the kitchen and the first-floor dining room, the kitchen can't see what's taking place at all ninety seats in the various dining rooms. The front-of-the-house staff, several members in particular, serve as the kitchen's eyes and ears.

In the eye of the storm is the restaurant's expediter, Erwin Sandoval, whose primary job is to hold the kitchen and the service team together. "I'm in the middle between the chefs and the servers. I keep track of the timing at all the tables and try to pace them from the kitchen. It's like putting a puzzle together every night because we are working with a variety of different situations," says Sandoval, a front-of-the-house staffer who wears a conservative blue suit amid a sea of white chef's jackets in the kitchen.

THE PIPER CALLS THE TUNES

The expediter needs to keep the engine on track and roaring ahead through an evening's usual thicket of complications. A dining room manager, for example, might tell Sandoval that four parties of guests who have arrived for the second seating are waiting for tables in the foyer-atrium bar. He would then to talk to chefs about accelerating the pace to more quickly produce food at tables that need to be released for the second seating. The restaurant has two seatings. On weeknights, the first seating begins at 6:00 and continues until 7:30. The second seating begins at 9:00 and guests will be seated until about 10:30.

A guest with a food allergy would prompt an adjustment in the remaining courses. "We have to be completely aware of a food allergy," says Sandoval. "If the server reports that someone has a shellfish allergy, I need to alert the chef to use a very, very clean cutting board and knife so no residue of an offending shellfish comes in contact with the food being served to that allergic guest. We take that very seriously."

Throughout the evening, Sandoval is visited by dining room managers and the floaters who patrol each floor. Servers, who generally remain in their dining room, will occasionally drop by the kitchen to report on activities at their tables. It's critical to get a sense for the guests' level of enthusiasm. A table that is psyched about the food or wine might be given an extra course. Adjustments might be needed at a table that doesn't seem to be warming to the experience.

Sandoval uses the intelligence gathered from the front-of-the-house staff to better orchestrate the flow in the back, much like an air traffic controller at a busy airport. When things don't click, he says there's the temptation to point fingers.

Sandoval smoothes over the rough edges. "I might go to a chef and say the mistake was the waiter's fault, but we have to move on." But Sandoval doesn't have much time to assuage wounded egos or negotiate front-back differences. The expediter has the final word.

At his side throughout the evening is Charlie Trotter, who essentially serves as an expediter along with Sandoval. Trotter inspects every dish before it leaves the kitchen, wiping the slightest hint of a smudge from the edge of the china. Dishes that don't meet his exacting standards go back with orders to get it right.

NOT CRAZY ABOUT SEA CUCUMBERS

Matt Merges says when a guest does send a dish back, neither he nor his team of chefs takes it personally. "I try to put myself in the guest's shoes," he says. "Not everything is to the guest's taste. But let's find out why. A foodstuff like sea cucumbers might seem too foreign. Rabbit might look too exotic. A dish might be too spicy. They might not like the texture of a dish like lamb's tongue. Our salmon might appear undercooked to a guest because only the protein is cooked at a temperature of 126 degrees. It's a wonderful cooking technique, but a server might have to explain that."

A chef might visit a table to offer his own explanation. "When a chef visits a table it allows the guest

"Service is the art of providing information to and fulfilling the needs of an individual or individuals. At Charlie Trotter's, service can be seen as a passion, a way of enhancing the food and wine journey. The service here is all about exceeding the guests' expectations, whether they are first-time guests or veterans of the restaurant. It is all about the little things that add up to the total package."

Matt Merges,
chef de cuisine and occasional
front-of-the-house staffer

to make a connection to the restaurant," says Merges. "It elevates the experience and is part of the whole package of things we can deliver here." He says it's also important to "challenge the guest in a cerebral way. Dining here is an opportunity for a guest to elevate his or her palate."

Merges and his staff work diligently to enlighten the palate and enhance the food knowledge of the front-of-the-house staff with tastings at Wednesday training sessions or with preservice samples of that evening's cuisine. Merges and members of his team always attend the service staff's preservice meeting to explain a dish, its ingredients, or perhaps where it came from. With a diverse, ever-changing menu, there's never a shortage of products to talk about.

"It's fascinating to watch how effortlessly they seem to coordinate their efforts with the kitchen. And what's most amazing is they are able to perform at that high level on a consistent basis. I have had great food at other restaurants, but if the service is missing a beat it diminishes the whole experience. Service is very important."

Charles Sitzes, a Chicagoan who has been dining at the restaurant since its earliest days

A MEASURE OF RESPECT

Merges says his staff has great respect for the front-of-the-house team, which has a strong command of the products leaving the kitchen. "They come in three hours before service begins, and they're here long after service is over. They work very hard in very tough circumstances."

That might explain why there's little resentment between the staffs, even when a server pushes the kitchen to its limits with complicated, customized requests. Sommelier Belinda Chang says that when she was a server she could drive the kitchen a bit crazy with her penchant for sending in orders that were tailored to meet a guest's tastes. But she doesn't recall any complaints directed at her because the kitchen realized the extra effort was well worth it. "The extra steps make the guest feel appreciated."

Dan Fitzgerald, a dining room manager, says the front-back synchronicity at Trotter's is remarkable. "The level of control and communication is unmatched."

Extra lines of defense help reduce the possibility of a service error. Marvin Godinez, coordinator of the food runners and server assistants, sees both ends of the house as he moves between the kitchen and the dining rooms throughout the night. "I can see certain situations developing in the kitchen or the dining room. I can then work with Erwin to make sure he's aware of the situations. I also pitch in at tables with food allergies to ensure that the person with the allergy is given the right plate. We are constantly communicating."

THE EYES HAVE IT

Communication—in both spoken and unspoken form—lies at the heart of the service team's success on the floor. Trotter, who is fond of sports metaphors, says coordination between service team members should be as flawless as the "no-look pass" perfected by the Los Angeles Lakers when they were led by Magic Johnson in the 1980s.

"Our servers can communicate with each other in a way that does not distract them when they are taking care of a guest," explains Mitchell Schmieding. "We do a lot with our eyes." And it would seem that some of them have an extra set in the back of their head as they glide through the room to pour wine, explain a dish, present a menu, clear a table, deliver plates of food, or escort a guest to the rest room.

Each of the three dining rooms features a lineup of two servers, a server assistant, and a sommelier. A manager who floats in and out of the room to lend a hand assists them throughout the evening. Teams of food runners help march the kitchen's handiwork to the tables.

LORDS OF THE DANCE

"Dining here is a beautifully choreographed event," says Mark Signorio. "If a guest gets up and places his or her napkin on the table, we will immediately replace it with a folded napkin. As you're taking the napkin off the table and walking to the service credenza, your teammate already has a new napkin in hand and is placing it on the table.

"It's all done so fleetingly and so quickly," he says. "People are truly touched by that kind of service. They get a big kick out of it." Food is to be delivered with the same sense of precision. "If you and your teammates have established a rhythm that evening the plates of food will be placed on the table in perfect sync. That's beautiful service that causes the guest to marvel and say, 'Wow.'"

Unlike the Lakers, who play to the roar of the crowd, the service team at Charlie Trotter's is quietly appreciated. "Our service is designed to be silent and seamless, but appreciated by the guests who sense that they are being carefully attended to," says Signorio. "For example, if you see a guest sneezing or their eyes watering, you go the rest room and return with a couple of tissues rather than approaching the table and asking the guest if he needs a tissue. The guest loves that kind of treatment."

SYNCHRONICITY

Trotter says the marriage between the service staff and the kitchen is a relatively happy one because there is no sharp distinction, as there often is at other restaurants, "between what is the kitchen and what is the dining room. I never liked it when I was working in a restaurant as a waiter or a busboy and the kitchen staff hated the dining room guys because they thought they were lazy and made a lot of money. And there were waiters who regarded the kitchen staff as a bunch of slimy lowlifes. They didn't even want to deal with them.

"But here it doesn't matter if you're wearing chef's whites or a dark suit. You're here to serve the great cause and remain focused on the big picture," says Trotter, who believes the perfectly orchestrated evening would be when every table is seemingly ecstatic. Wines that perfectly match the cuisine would accompany the cuisine, which would be meticulously prepared. The food and wine would be served in a timely manner. The service would be impeccable, and the dining room would crackle with kinetic energy—a great vibe.

And how often has the restaurant achieved such a state of ecstasy? "Maybe once in fourteen years," Trotter says matter of factly. "For that to happen, everything has to be working in concert. The whole has to be greater than the sum of its parts. It's something that is almost intangible."

Yet Trotter believes lightning can and will strike twice if he and the staff integrate the right elements. One of the most problematic elements of the dining mix is the dynamic of the room. It is influenced by such factors as a guest's mood, a guest's expectations of the evening, how people are seated in the room, or how guests at one table may perceive what is taking place at another table.

"Working the dining room is like a complicated game of chess," says Trotter. "You're thinking about all the strategic moves that need to be made—services to perform for the guests before they even realize they want them."

CONTROLLING A WILDFIRE

But a dining room can be as mercurial as quicksilver. "Some nights it just doesn't click," says Signorio. "The weather may be causing problems. People are late. A guest may be miserable because he or she is there only because of a spouse. You may have tried every trick in the book to get that table to come around. You don't write that table off, but you want to know where that table is at. If you let a table get out of control, it can spark a chain reaction. For example, one table overhears a person at another table complaining about something and then everyone is unhappy. It can be contagious in both a negative way and a positive way."

Sometimes, the most noble service touches can prompt a negative reaction. "If we bring a special dish to one table, people at another table wonder why they're not getting the same thing," says Signorio. "We might have made the special dish because the person has an allergy or it could be because it's a guest who has dined with us many times before. If the server sensed that guests at another table felt shortchanged or if they complained outright about unbalanced treatment, he would order the special dish for them as well. It's a fine balance in the dining room. We're all very conscious of that."

There is a different dynamic at each table in the room, says senior server Paul Larson. "You might have a single diner who has never been here before, and you sense they are a little uncomfortable sitting there by themselves. We might offer them a book to read. If they are interested in a conversation, we'll spend some extra time at the table talking to them. Every situation is different."

STRANGE BEDFELLOWS IN THE DINING ROOM

Kurt Sorensen says there's no way to predict the dining room dynamics on any given evening. "That's because there is no typical diner here. There may be people in the room who have saved their money for a year to come and celebrate their thirtieth wedding anniversary. It may be the only time they will ever be here. There are diners who come here every two or three months, and then there are the sophisticated world travelers, perhaps a couple who might make the point that they came from Germany to dine in the restaurant. You might have that mix in the dining room, one table right next to the other."

Guests at Trotter's often pay careful attention to their fellow diners. It's all part of the entertainment. "It's not just about dining, but it's what other people are doing at their table. So a server plays each table as if it were a chess game so one table does not feel more important or less significant than the other even though some guests have ordered $400 and $500 bottles of wine and another table may be drinking water," says Sorensen. "If someone orders a rather expensive bottle of wine, we might choose to order an extra course to match that bottle of wine. And we might bring some oversized wine glasses to their table. But the other table might want to know why they got the extra course or the big glasses."

To better manage the individual dynamic at each table, the server needs to adjust his or her personality, says Sorensen. "You certainly don't want to be a chameleon by changing your colors at each table, but you need to be flexible as to how you respond and meet the needs of each table. If there's a table that's having a hard time engaging in conversation, I might listen for key words. If they say they're from Florida, I might say my fellow server, Jason, lived in Florida. We then have something in common and the ice is broken. By connecting with the dining room, I can sometimes make a guest feel more comfortable, which is the ultimate goal."

The dynamic of the dining room, says Sorensen, "can be played between guest and guest, guest and server, and kitchen and guest. It takes incredible planning."

SEEKING THE RIGHT CHEMISTRY

The planning, says Trotter, takes place from several standpoints. "It happens from the expediting post in the kitchen as to how the food is timed and how it flows into the dining room. It happens from the reservations system and the front door as to how people are seated. There is a dynamic that can be created by seating certain kinds of tables together. It happens through conversations between the servers and the kitchen during the course of the evening. The servers might say: 'These people are having a great time. They want more food, so let's draw out the evening for them.' Another server might say: 'My table wants to go faster, so let's condense the evening.'"

Trotter says that from the casual observer's perspective, "one night would appear no different from the next night. But from our standpoint, every night is really very different because of the nature of the people who come here, their expectations as well as the timing of the food and how well we pull it all together."

There's a science to the seating at Trotter's, which has three dining rooms, plus the studio kitchen and the table in the kitchen. "Logically, you would seat the first table in the downstairs dining room, the second table would go upstairs in the back salon, the third table will go up in the balcony dining room, we'd put the fourth table back downstairs, and so on."

FILLING NO ROOM BEFORE ITS TIME

They could seat people "so there is an even demand for each dining room and no one on the service team is overwhelmed," says Trotter. "But when you do that, you end up halfway through the night with three rooms that are only half to three-quarters filled."

Instead, one dining room is filled at a time to "create energy and a dynamic and a mood. It may not be the easiest way to do it from the service staff's perspective because they are deluged with service needs in that room. But on the other hand, it better suits the guests. Part of the dining experience is to be able to see other people. Even if you're not looking directly at them, you are able to feel them around you. You might hear the faint hint of a conversation at the table next to you."

Trotter says people dine out ostensibly to gaze into a companion's eyes or to toast a significant event, but the presence of other guests is a critical element in the overall experience.

A crowded dining room won't necessarily guarantee a positive flow of energy. "You can have a room full of people, but it is deadly silent. But on the other hand, you walk into some rooms and you can literally walk one foot above the ground because the energy is so strong."

A METHOD TO THE MADNESS

There are numerous subtleties to seating the guests—or arranging the pieces on the chessboard—explains Trotter. If the intelligence has been gathered properly, the reservationist and the front door staff will know to put certain returning guests at certain tables in the restaurant. "We might know that Mr. Smith, for example, prefers to eat slowly and he likes to talk to people at the neighboring table so maybe we'd better put him at a table where he's not too close to someone."

Trotter's reservationist prepares a computer printout of the guests' names and times they plan to arrive a week ahead. But the reservation chart is far from complete. The chart will go through several revisions as people cancel and others are added. By 5 P.M., shortly before service begins, the front door staff is working off what they call "the static sheet," that evening's rough blueprint.

"We challenge ourselves to exceed a guest's expectations of the food, wine, ambiance and, of course, service. We do that by interviewing the guest in the course of a conversation. It can last from the start to the finish of the evening. At the start of the conversation, we gather information about dietary restrictions, allergies, and any dislikes to certain foods. We do more listening and observing as the conversation evolves through the evening. There is no ceiling to the service we can provide."

Debra Torres, server

If there is a cancellation or a no-show after 5 P.M., a manager will make a note of it on the sheet and alert Trotter. Explains a dining room manager, "If we're expecting 120 people and a party of four cancels and two people no-show, we might be able to add a party of two or a party of four (the most common party size is two). They could be people who have been calling for a month hoping to get in at the last minute or it might be a concierge trying to work in a guest from a hotel. It's a dynamic system that allows you to move things around."

Guests from the first seating who linger at their tables can throw a wrench into the works when the second seating arrives, but the front door staff can almost always adjust the evening's seating chart to avoid a backup in the foyer-atrium bar. Logistics have an enormous bearing on the dynamics of that evening's service.

BEHAVIORS IN A HUMAN LABORATORY

Yet the evening's careful planning can be frustrated by the vagaries of human behavior that play out on the floor, says Trotter, recalling an evening when guests reported having a wonderful time, with one small exception. A man at the next table kept muttering negative things under his breath. It marred the evening for the guests, who were invited to come back for another meal. On another night, a guest dining at the kitchen table suffered an epileptic seizure and collapsed in the kitchen doorway. The delivery of food to the dining rooms was halted for nearly an hour to allow time for the paramedics to arrive and treat the man.

There have been times when a guest behaving obnoxiously disrupted the dining room dynamic. A guest's ringing cell phone has rudely interrupted; vulgar language has been used within earshot of other tables. It is rare to have one guest ask another to tone it down or clean it up, and it can set off an ugly reaction. Servers or Trotter himself will step in to restore civility. "You have to be able to conform or adjust for so many varieties of guests. You never know what you are going to get yourself into. But that's the beauty of fluid and flexible service."

His service team prepares to deal with the unexpected twists and turns on the floor through role playing. "You can't think of enough scenarios because so many different things can happen. But if you present enough of them in a training session, employees can extrapolate certain lessons and learn how to deal with them."

Over the years, Trotter has tweaked the calculus of the dining room by "firing" certain categories of guests because they or their tastes were no longer appropriate for the restaurant's mission. The first to go were diners who preferred to dine à la carte when Trotter's switched to a degustation menu. Next were the smokers, whose cigarettes polluted the dining room, and the most recent to go were guests who like a cocktail in the bar or with a meal. Why make great food for people with numbed palates? Trotter figured.

For service to truly succeed, the guest must be an active participant in the dining experience. "The service staff member must be eager and focused on providing extraordinary service, but the guest is almost as responsible. The guest has to be able to receive and appreciate the experience. You just can't beat someone over the head with great food, great wine, great ambiance, and great service," says Trotter. "And there are times when a guest is psyched for a great experience and we are incapable of delivering on all cylinders." It takes two to tango.

If the dance is to work, servers at Charlie Trotter's need to be keen observers. Signorio says he learns a lot about a table once he steps back and watches the guest's reactions to a dish or a glass of wine. If the guest seemed pleased, Signorio would usually stay put. But if he sensed that a guest was unhappy with something, he would step forward and offer to take an item back to the kitchen in favor of something else.

"Everything is poised, unhurried, and in focus in these elegant salons. Trotter's long procession of small lapidary-perfect dishes are innovative, often improvisational, yet always harmonious. Meals last up to four hours. Book the kitchen table far ahead."

Chicago *magazine*

"You can get a more honest expression as you step back into the weeds. I would position myself in a way that I could hear what they are saying about the food. It's eavesdropping, but not in a malicious way. For example, a guest might say 'I wish I had ordered the vegetable menu instead of the grand.' I would then run to the kitchen and switch the menu from the grand to the vegetable menu without even talking to them.

"Or I might hear a guest say that she's a little reluctant about a particular course. So I'll go to the kitchen and request a special course for that guest to try. I'll bring it to the table and explain that I've had something specially prepared for you and that you're welcome to try something other than this. They are very impressed by that because of what I was able to do for them."

While it's important to anticipate a guest's needs, it's equally important not to prejudge a guest. "You walk a fine line because if your assessment of a table is wrong you can be in dangerous territory," says Signorio, who's made the mistake of being lighthearted and friendly with guests who were serious and reserved. His attempt to break the ice at that table with a bit of humor was a misfire.

On another occasion, he misread a couple dining in the restaurant. The man was in a rumpled seersucker suit and the woman in a simple-looking dress. The couple ordered a $5,000 bottle of wine and Trotter then prepared a special multicourse meal for them. "That reminded me that I have no right to make assumptions about a guest or approach their table with some preconceived notions."

BACK STAGE AT CHARLIE TROTTER'S

The biggest mistake a server can make is to be perceived by a guest as condescending about his or her command of the cuisine in the presence of another guest, says Signorio. Despite the staff's efforts to treat guests with sincerity and a Midwestern warmth, some detractors say that the service is pretentious.

THE NATURAL

Misreads of customers and other mistakes will happen in an environment where the servers are encouraged to be themselves rather than robotically approach a table with some carefully rehearsed script. Service at Charlie Trotter's is not overproduced nor does it suffer from an overbearing formality. "We encourage our servers to be their own person on the floor," says Mitchell Schmieding. "There isn't one particular way of presenting a menu or describing a dish or a particular wine. Each server is allowed to do it in a way that best suits him or her."

The problem with drilling the staff with rehearsed presentations or responses is that it robs the service of its warmth and naturalness, says Schmieding. Even more troubling is that staff members may not actually know what they're talking about. "If a server has just given a rehearsed presentation about a roulet of salmon and someone asks him what that means and he doesn't know, it could be very embarrassing."

Overly produced or overly rehearsed service would undermine the spontaneity and common-sense resourcefulness that servers are expected to practice in the dining room. The best servers have an almost sixth sense for their guests' needs. "A good server should be able to walk through the dining room and catch a guest's eyes and sense that something is up. If a guest looks up from a conversation, there's usually something that needs attention at that table. It should all be seamless and flawless," says Schmieding.

THE RULES OF THE ROAD

Underpinning the unique dining room choreography at Charlie Trotter's is a communication system that is largely based on a set of unwritten rules that have become second nature to the service staff. New hires come to adopt the rules during their initial months of informal, earn-while-you-learn training.

For example, if a pair of servers, each armed with two plates of food, approach a four-top table, the first server goes to the farthest position and delivers his plates. That avoids a potential collision at the table with the trailing server, who puts his plates at the nearest position. Another example, says Schmieding, is that a good server will instinctively know not to clear a table until every guest has completed his or her meal. When that time comes, service team members will simply catch each other's eyes and move in to clear.

Another important unwritten rule is that the guest always has the right of way in the restaurant. After that service staffers running food have precedence over a staffer carrying empty plates or glasses.

READING THE TEA LEAVES

Sari Zernich, an office staffer who tests the restaurant's recipes, says she's amazed by the front-of-the-house staff's ability to read the guests' minds. It was a phenomenon she observed the first time she dined at the restaurant. "The service is quiet and so subtle but it's so far ahead of the game," says Zernich.

"For Trotter, each dish is a piece on the chessboard that must be considered in relation to other dishes on the menu. They're designed to be eaten completely without leaving diners to stumble off uncomfortably full. In addition, each move in the kitchen implies a new wine possibility. Though the combinations are endlessly intricate, servers operate strictly from memory."

Restaurant Business

Actually, the reservationist makes a daily seating chart, including all relevant comments about a particular guest. The sheet is then transferred to reservation books kept in the atrium-foyer, the upstairs dining room, and the kitchen. Managers and servers will have foreknowledge about the guests before they arrive. The comments are written in a shorthand code that all service staff members can quickly decipher. For example, "MBD" indicates that the guest must be seated in the downstairs dining room.

A FAILURE TO COMMUNICATE

Mishandling internal communications can lead to a guest's disappointment. Trotter employees are encouraged to enjoy a sort of busman's holiday during vacations or days off by dining in other restaurants. One service staffer recalled how he explained to the reservationist at one of San Francisco's top restaurants that he wanted the staff to select the wines for his meal. The reservationist assured him that would be no problem. But when he arrived at the restaurant and was seated at his table, a waiter brought him a wine list. Puzzled, he told the waiter that he made arrangements for them to select the wines. The waiter said he was unaware of any such plans. The left hand had no knowledge of what the right hand was doing.

The restaurant's dropped hand-off left a bad taste in the employee's mouth, who said the incident reminded him of how well Charlie Trotter's strives to communicate both among its staff and to its guests. "If anything, I think we overcommunicate at this restaurant," says the employee, who notes Trotter's fondness for the phrase: "Remind me to the point where I'm irritated with you."

EXTRA LAYERS OF PROTECTION

Communication at Charlie Trotter's is more difficult than at restaurants with a single dining room. "Communications are trickier here," says Trotter. "It means our managers have to float around a bit more. I don't see that as a negative because if we had a single dining room this would not be the same restaurant. It would not have the same level of intimacy."

But the physical obstacles are overcome by the staff's many-layered communications system—from advance information to on-the-spot observation and constant teamwork—that's designed to ultimately deliver what Trotter calls "beautiful, flawless, and spontaneous service. We're all trying to do this unique thing, and what we do is very special."

SERVICE POINTS

To better meld the talents of separate divisions or departments within a business, consider these service points:

- Assign someone to quickly resolve any disputes the way Trotter's uses an expediter to help knit the service and kitchen teams together.

- Share information and intelligence between teams so they can satisfy their mutual customer.

- Have staff members train their counterparts; cross training helps reduce interdepartmental resentment and misunderstandings.

- Members of another team should not feel uncomfortable or be made to feel guilty about requesting something extra in the name of a satisfied customer.

- Use role playing exercises to better prepare employees for unanticipated developments.

- Prepare a game plan, but be prepared to change it on a moment's notice.

- "Fire" customers who no longer fit in with your mission. Customer misbehavior will alienate your good customers.

- Establish nonverbal means of communication: Body language and facial expressions can be used to send messages and supplement regular channels.

- Teach employees to anticipate the needs of customers.

- Let employees be themselves when communicating with customers. Rehearsed presentations to customers sound insincere.

- Remind colleagues and managers of important matters frequently. It's better to overcommunicate than to drop the ball.

- Create a shorthand code that the staff can instantly decipher to speed up and streamline internal communications.

8

On Murphy's Law and
the Rules of Recovery

Stuff happens, and when it does, a business had better be ready to deal with the consequences. Charlie Trotter's is quick to make amends when its service falls short. And thanks to its customer satisfaction surveys, the restaurant can constantly monitor its performance and make whatever corrections are necessary.

Charlie Trotter says it's hard to savor the accomplishments of his restaurant when he's humbled each day by its shortcomings.

When asked what the restaurant could be doing better, he replies, "Do you have a few hours?" There's plenty that can and will go wrong in a restaurant where 120 to 130 guests come five nights a week expecting the dining experience of a lifetime. They usually get it, but not always.

Chicago's notorious weather, which can delay guests' arrivals, can always throw a wrench in the works of an operation that's expected to run like a Swiss watch. Guests can arrive harried or in a fractious mood. Staff members can call in sick, stretching the service team thin. Some of those on hand may be fatigued or lacking the laser-sharp focus they're expected to bring with them each night.

And then there's the "sandpile," the small glitches that compound each other.

For example, guests who stay longer than expected during the first seating delay the second seating, which begins about 9 P.M. Incoming guests are left to cool their heels in the foyer-atrium bar. "You don't want it to become a mosh pit of angry people," says one staffer. A table might take an unusually long time understanding the menu, delaying a server from tending to another of his tables. A dish may not be to a guest's liking. That dish and, as per policy, every other guest's dish at that table then go back to the kitchen for a replating. That may set the clock back ten minutes. And the dominoes continue to fall despite the service staff's best efforts.

THE ENLIGHTENING LESSONS OF FAILURE

But what separates the good restaurants from the truly great is how they correct a mistake and learn from it. "Success is great, but I've had innumerable failures," says Trotter, who pushes himself and his staff to learn and gracefully recover from mistakes—both big and small. According to the restaurant's unwritten rules of recovery, the first step calls for an honest and sincere apology to the guest. The next step is to resolve the problem.

A simple apology is often the best compensation when a business has let a customer down. Not apologizing may further disappoint or anger a customer who's soon to become an ex-customer. And a begrudging or long-delayed apology is as good as no apology at all. If Trotter's screws up big-time, it's Trotter himself who delivers the apology and begins mending fences.

Francisco Estrada, a veteran server assistant at the restaurant, says he once spilled coffee on a man's suit. "I felt terrible and apologized several times. But the guest was understanding. I gave him my business card and told him that I wanted him to send me the dry cleaning bill so we could pay for it." Despite the spill, the man told

Estrada that he managed to enjoy his meal and chose not to take Estrada up on his offer. Like Trotter says, it's how gracefully you can recover from a mistake.

But mistakes happen. During a Wednesday training meeting, some of the servers were shaking their heads over a series of missteps the night before. "I wish the food runners were still in the room to hear this," said Jason Platt, a server. "They were consistently serving the wrong plates on table 45. We looked like the Keystone Kops." Marvin Godinez, who coordinates the food runners and servers' assistants, did not attempt to defend their miscues. "That never should have happened," he said. "But we have to remember to repeat the table numbers and say them clearly. Table 33 can sound a lot like table 43, for example."

"Even the smallest mistake can get magnified at Charlie Trotter's," says Mark Signorio. "There is the money dynamic. It's an expensive place, and people want to make sure they're getting everything they're entitled to. The tough part here is that guests expect perfection or whatever their definition of it is. For

"Attentive service is as much an art form as the culinary arts that are practiced in the kitchen. If a diner has to ask for more water, wine, or a fresh napkin, the staff has already failed. A waiter must understand the timeline of a guest's meal. Equally important is the ability of the service staff to remain 'invisible' throughout the evening. It's placing another roll on a plate or refilling a glass without the guest even noticing. Over-service is just as bad as under-service, such as when the server refills the glass each time the customer takes a sip. The constant invasion of a guest's space interrupts the flow of the evening for the guest. Good servers are discreet."

Jason Smith, assistant sommelier

example, we aim to serve our courses twenty minutes apart, but if we did one course twenty-two minutes later, that may be short of the guest's standard.

"I think that's one reason we are much more conscientious about people's needs," says Signorio. "A wait is a wait, but we need to do everything possible to make that guest feel more comfortable. Most restaurants wouldn't dream of giving away free champagne unless it was a crisis situation. Here, we'll often say, 'We're sorry that you had to wait ten minutes. The champagne is on us.'"

ROLLING WITH THE PUNCHES

"Sometimes guests will show up early, oddly enough on nights when the weather is poor. They think the driving conditions will be worse than they actually are and end up here fifty minutes before a 9 P.M. reservation," says Signorio. "By the time you seat them at 9:10, they'll complain that they had to wait an hour. But do you remind them that they were here nearly an hour early? No."

It's possible, he says, to unconsciously make a mistake at a table. A guest might, for example, misinterpret a server's sense of humor and mistake the server's tone as patronizing. "There are a million ways you can insult a customer, and sometimes you're not even aware of it. Once you sense that you may have insulted them, you retreat, you change your personality. At that point the guest may no longer trust you. He or she will no longer take any of your suggestions. All you can really do is simply become a server at that table in the strictest sense of the term and take all the emotion out of the relationship. It's a bad situation."

"Service follows a classic pattern, never hurried, but always on top of things. The general tone was quiet, poised, serene. All the excitement was on the plate or in the glass."

Wine Spectator

The best damage control strategy is to be "superattentive to the guests. I make sure that everything is absolutely perfect at the table. I am there when every course is served. But there's a lot of pressure at that point. The guests may become highly judgmental of everything you do, and there's the possibility they will put a complaint in on you." Providing the upset guests an extra course might be perceived as bribery and make things all the worse. "That works, but only after you have reconnected with the guest. The best way to do that is to be honest and say 'I'm sorry I upset you.'"

SEEKING ANTIDOTES TO TROUBLE

Most sticky situations can be salvaged with a bit of extra hustle and teamwork, says Signorio. Trouble could be brewing in the foyer-atrium bar, where guests may have had to wait forty-five minutes. "At that point they're staring daggers at the front-door staff." Alerted to the delay and the guests' state of mind by the front-door staff, he would then launch a recovery operation. He would first tell the other server in the room that a particular table will need to be watched very closely.

"We might offer them free champagne to begin the course. I would ask the other server in that dining room to brief the guests on the menu while I run down to the kitchen and ask that they start a special amuse course for the table. It's important to get food in the mouth of a guest who has experienced a delay. That helps break down the wait time and gets the dining experience underway." Signorio will also work with the kitchen to put the guests' first course on the fast track to further limit the delay. The server can do just about anything it takes to get the evening back on track for the guests.

There are times when a guest is the culprit. Loud or obnoxious guests can sometimes disturb diners at other tables within the restaurant's intimate confines. On one occasion, a guest walked over

147

to a table to ask those guests to please lower their voices. An argument erupted between the two tables before the service staff could swoop in and calm things down. The spat disturbed every diner in the room.

A fruit fly once marred the evening for a guest. Despite the restaurant's well-polished, antiseptically clean kitchen, a fruit fly found its way into a guest's wine glass. In the customer satisfaction survey, the guest said he could understand how a fruit fly could find its way into a glass. What truly concerned him, however, was his server's reaction. He wrote that the server immediately removed the glass, and he was apologetic. But he asked the guest how he'd prefer to see the restaurant make amends. The guest wrote that he felt like he was being put on the spot and that the server should have been more assertive about resolving the situation.

The incident served as the basis of an intense discussion in a preservice meeting and at a Wednesday afternoon training session. Trotter's message to the staff was simple. Take charge. Don't leave it up to a customer as to how a mistake should be resolved.

MAKING THE SYSTEM FAULT TOLERANT

Mitchell Schmieding acts as a sort of safety net during the evening as he floats between the first-floor dining room and the foyer-atrium bar. "I'm not one to walk through the dining room and put out fires," he says. "I prefer to foresee what can possibly happen before something actually does." And it always does. "There is going to be human error. We are working with the unbelievably unpredictable."

He likens the floater position to having an extra pilot in the cockpit of an aircraft. "Service would be relatively flawless without the floater, but it is an extra layer of checks and balances," says Schmieding. The floater position differs from a traditional manager's position at other restaurants because a manager rarely leaves the front door. A floater is assigned to both floors of the restaurant and, unlike a traditional manager, a floater will pitch in on everything from a major crisis to the seemingly most ordinary of tasks. A floater might top off a water glass, tidy up a rest room, hail taxis, hang coats, or replace the butter at a table. He makes frequent visits to the kitchen. "Like a lot of things here," says Schmieding, "the floater position evolved over time."

Problems he sees most commonly on the floor include mis-serving food, a guest not getting the wine he ordered, an extended wait for food, or a guest being annoyed by another guest in the room. Schmieding steps in when a situation at one table is taking an excessive amount of a server's time. Without a service backstop, the sandpile begins to grow and guests at other tables are shortchanged by a lack of service. Discontented guests begin to grumble.

"Hopefully, the net result is that the other guests don't get the impression that they are not being taken care of," says Schmieding. When something goes awry on the floor, server Christian Giles says, "we only compound our mistake if

"Members of the service team are careful listeners. One evening, for example, I casually said to a server that I didn't think the restaurant would ever be the same because sommelier Larry Stone was planning to leave. On a visit to the restaurant several months later, Charlie Trotter dropped by my table and said he understood that I had some concerns about the restaurant's future. He said he wanted to assure me that each meal we had would be better than the last one we had. That told me how seriously he takes into account his guests' opinions. We all feel that we are treated very special by Charlie and his staff."

Dan Mjolsness, Chicago-based executive who has been a guest chef-for-the-day on three occasions

149

we stomp our feet in disgust or complain out loud to the other server in the room." Likewise, if a glass or a plate falls to the ground, "we shouldn't go running out of the room to see what happened. It only makes the problem more evident to the guest."

Schmieding says good service, the occasional flaw notwithstanding, is what keeps the restaurant's other three pillars (food, wine, and ambiance) in balance. "By that I mean you could have a poor dinner or a mediocre dinner, but with great service you will still walk away saying it was an enjoyable experience. But if the service is lacking and the food is superlative, you've lost. Service is what keeps the experience in balance because it is an emotional transaction. How often are people taken care of in a sincere manner? Not very often.

"That's why if there is a complication with the food or a problem with the service, we will apologize and do whatever we can to take care of it," says Schmieding. "A swift response makes all the difference in the world. The guest will likely quickly forget about the problem because of a positive reaction by the staff."

TROUBLESHOOTING

The restaurant also backstops against serving a guest a food item that will trigger an allergic reaction. Marvin Godinez will keep a watchful eye on tables where there are allergic alerts. The kitchen, the server, and the floater have been made ware of the alert, but Godinez is the last line of defense. Missing an alert "is one of the worst things that can happen here. It could endanger a guest's health."

Little mistakes, Marvin Godinez says, can snowball into big problems. "If we were told by a man that he was here to celebrate his wife's birthday and we miss the cue, the night turns out to be a big disappointment. Every guest comes here with huge expectations and it's up to us to not only live up to those expectations, but to go beyond them."

Signorio says quickly addressing or resolving a negative experience for guests makes them feel that they've been listened to in a sincere manner. "But if it's a negative experience and you just send them on their way, their only way to come to terms with it is to share with other people how bad an experience it was. Word of mouth can be very damaging to a restaurant.

"When we get a complaint about something we've done wrong, we act on it quickly and in a constructive manner. We don't tell people they were wrong. Regardless of whether it's a legitimate complaint, it's still a legitimate disappointment for the guest."

THE TRUTH HURTS

And when guests are disappointed, Trotter wants to know about it.

"You have to listen to the negative comments, because if you don't it's devastating. If you don't know what you're doing wrong, how can you correct it?" Trotter listens carefully to what the customer has to say through a variety of channels, but the most effective and most measurable is the customer satisfaction survey that is presented to each table at the end of the evening.

About 90 percent of the evaluations and accompanying comments are glowing. Those are the surveys that check "yes" to the question: "Do you plan to join us again in the future?" A second category of responding guests—about 5 to 6 percent—indicate that they had a delightful evening but do not plan to return. They might be from out of town, they may have thought the meal was too expensive, or they may like to sample a variety of fine dining venues.

The final group is the one that merits Trotter's closest attention. It's the 4 or 5 percent of guests who indicate on the survey that they don't plan to return because of some flaw in the evening. Reasons cited may include complaints about the cuisine, too long a wait at the door, too long a period between courses, or a server who was perceived to be too snooty.

"WHERE DID WE GO WRONG?"

Trotter examines every survey that is returned. Nearly three-fourths of the guests will take the time to rate the food, the wine list, their server, and the rest of the service staff on a scale of 1 (poor) to 5 (outstanding). In addition to the ranking, guests are invited to comment on each category. There are also open-ended questions, such as: "What could we have done to improve your experience?"

"Good service requires 'court vision.' Like a great basketball player, you have to see everything in the field of play and be able to respond before it actually happens. You are at your best when you are listening carefully to your guest. At other restaurants, a server might overhear a guest complain that something is not to their liking and do nothing about it. That would not happen here. We do things without ever being asked by a guest to do them."

Rene Roman, server

A manager will call a guest who indicated that he or she was not satisfied with the experience. If the complaint is egregious, Trotter will personally make the call and attempt to find out what went wrong. "It's been said before, but a complaint is a gift. We thank our lucky stars that someone took the time to let us know that we have a problem. We can fix a problem, and we can become permanently better at what we do because of the complaint."

Although it can be disheartening, even painful, to learn from a customer that you're not doing things to his or her satisfaction, Trotter prefers to look at the complaint more positively. "Failures are worth more than successes. You learn more from those experiences. You work for success, but it's the failures that will help you get to the next success."

Trotter says he can't understand why so few businesses in America use customer satisfaction surveys. Although the hotel industry extensively uses customer satisfaction surveys, the forms themselves are often placed in low-visibility locations in guests' rooms—as if the hotel is not genuinely interested in their feedback, says Trotter. When customer surveys are done right, "They can be a great way to keep your hand on the pulse of your business."

Customer satisfaction surveys take some work. Trotter's gets a high response rate because the trifold surveys can fit easily into a pocket, and they are already stamped with return postage. About half the forms are filled out and left at the table; the other half are taken home. Guests usually mail surveys back within two weeks of their visit, although Trotter has fielded some that were completed two years after the guest's visit. He keeps a stack of the completed surveys on a windowsill of his second-floor office.

MAKING THINGS RIGHT

Once he's reviewed the surveys, Trotter will pass some of them along to such managers as Mitchell Schmieding, Dan Fitzgerald, or the restaurant's chef de cuisine, Matt Merges. If a guest has raised a concern, a manager will call the guest to learn more or simply to apologize. In some cases, a manager might send a gift bag or a cookbook to a guest to demonstrate that the restaurant was sincerely interested in his or her complaint. At least twice a month, a guest who raised a serious concern in the survey will be invited to return with his or her party so Trotter's can prove that it can provide an extraordinary evening for them. The meals are on the house, which means it comes right out of the bottom line. But Trotter feels it's a wise investment in the restaurant's well-tended reputation.

Christian Giles coordinates the distribution of the survey forms each evening. He encourages his colleagues to personalize the surveys by writing the guest's name at the top of the form. Leaving nothing to chance, the spelling of the guest's name is verified against the name that appears on the guest's credit card. Every three months, each server is given a stack of all the surveys that evaluated that server's performance.

"It's a sort of report card for us," says Giles. "They're helpful because they let us see patterns. It could be something we weren't aware of. If there's a problem, a manager will pull the server aside and discuss ways to remedy it." Critical comments about a server's performance on a survey or surveys can be tough to swallow because, as Giles says, "We take our jobs very seriously."

TALKING POINTS

Trotter or one of his managers will often bring surveys to the pre-service meeting, where no holds are barred when discussing a shortcoming raised in a survey. Although Trotter or a manager won't usually name the server who's the focus of a customer complaint, the table number is often identified, which is tantamount to identifying the server.

It's not done to be punitive, says Mark Signorio. "A critical survey will be discussed as a way of raising everyone's consciousness about a problem. It makes us stronger as a team. It's better to deal with a problem than it is to deny it. There are usually a positive cause and effect." Letters of praise are also aired at staff meetings, and those names are named.

Trotter says the surveys are a source of enlightenment for him, the managers, and the service staff. He suggests that businesses implementing a similar customer feedback program share the results with several layers of management. At Trotter's, a negative letter is always shared with an employee, usually behind closed doors. "We often couch it in a way that will not overwhelm the individual," says Trotter.

"Day in and day out, our people get a lot of well-deserved praise. I think employees understand that there are times when a negative comment comes through. The survey might say, for example, that the guest didn't like the attitude of the server, or he or she felt talked down to by the server. I'll call the server in and ask what happened at that table. The server might explain that the guests misinterpreted his use of humor as sarcastic or arrogant. I then have a little more information when I call the guest back. There is room for misinterpretation. And frankly, there have been occasions when the guest was just being a jerk about it."

Nevertheless, Trotter listens, and listens carefully. Fishing a recently returned survey from the stack in his office, Trotter pores over it in search of useful information. On this particular form, the guest indicated that he was pleased with the wine selection and applauded his server for customizing a cross between the grand and the vegetable menus. The guest declared the food to be innovative and perfectly cooked. However, the guest did note that he felt that each course delivery was interrupted because the server explained each dish when it arrived at the table.

"It became annoying," wrote the guest. "Why didn't he ask beforehand whether we wanted the dish

"Trotter is a cross between jazz great Duke Ellington and a military commander. On the one hand, there is this strict sense of discipline like an army, yet there is a sense of flexibility that only a jazz artist is capable of. They can make an adjustment to any type of situation in the dining room. I have seen Charlie walk through the dining room and notice, for example, a plate that has not been cleared, and he'll shoot a glance to a server who will immediately respond."

Ray Harris, Wall Street financier who has eaten at Charlie Trotter's nearly 300 times

explained before he delivered it? Thank you." Trotter says he found the letter valuable because he's read similar complaints from other guests. But it's a tough call, he says. "The same server can explain the same set of courses to two separate tables. One table might complain that they got too much information and the other table just the opposite."

SEIZING ON NUANCES

Based on the surveys, Trotter decided some fine-tuning was in order. He discussed the surveys at a preservice meeting and pointed out that servers must walk a fine line between guests who want an explanation of the dishes and those who simply want the food dropped off at their tables. "What the surveys were telling us was that maybe we should simply ask what the table wants instead of assuming that each table wants an explanation. The letters didn't necessarily prompt a change in policy, but they did heighten our awareness. We needed to a better job of picking up on signals. That's how subtly we have to look at our guests."

Trotter pulled out another survey form in which the guest wrote that he and his wife were "outraged" that the sommelier selected a $180 bottle of wine for their meal. The guest wrote that no price was ever discussed, and he was appalled when the bill was presented. He was expecting that the wine would have cost about half as much. The guest, who had dined at Trotter's several times over the years, was so upset that he wanted his name removed from the restaurant's mailing list.

Trotter says that particular poor service complaint was one that he personally handled. First, he called in sommelier Belinda Chang. She explained that she had served the guests in the past, and they had been comfortable with wine in the $180 price range. They had been pleased with her previous recommendations. On past visits, they had never voiced a concern about a $180 bottle of wine.

MAKING AN HONEST MISTAKE

Trotter now realizes that such an assumption may have been a mistake, and in the future, nothing will be left to misinterpretation. Prices or price ranges on wine will be firmly agreed upon, regardless of how well a staff person knows the guests' tastes. "I called them and told them I feel badly that this happened to them, especially as they've been coming here for years," says Trotter. "I told them it was an honest mistake on our part. We always accept full responsibility. We are not going to make excuses. I invited them to return as our guests."

The guest considered the invitation and called Trotter several days later to say that he and his wife would return but declined Trotter's offer to pick up the tab. "We served them an amazing meal," says Trotter. He instructed the server to present them a note at the end of the evening indicating that there would be no charge for the meal. But Trotter's generous gesture backfired. "They were irate, insulted that we would not allow them to pay for the meal. We're damned if we do and damned if we don't. We're probably the only restaurant in the United States that comps a $450 dining experience and angers the customer," he noted with a wry sense of resignation.

Making amends is usually far less complicated, says Trotter, who will attempt to get an elaboration on the complaint. "I or a manager will apologize. I'll tell them that I know they came for a certain reason and with high expectations that were not met. Please give us the opportunity to prove that the decision they made was the right one. Only once or twice has someone refused to come back."

Trotter has also called some guests simply to thank them for their letter that gushed with praise. That kind of call is usually in response to a letter that goes into great detail about extraordinary service or how exquisite the meal was. Trotter will often reinforce his gratitude with a cookbook or a set of videotapes of his PBS cooking series.

GIVE ME FEEDBACK

Comments are critical in the survey form, says Trotter. Some guests give the staff and kitchen all 5s, which is flattering but not terribly useful. He would rather get personal comments—good, bad, or otherwise. "A lot of people are nonconfrontational," he says. "They might have been unhappy with the dining experience. They might be at the point of never coming back or of badmouthing the restaurant. But as they walk out the door, they tell you everything was fine. You can't read them."

The survey form is often more telling. The guest might indicate that he or she thought the meal was overpriced, that one of the dishes was undercooked or too salty, or that the wait was overly long between courses. The survey form allows guests to provide a candid, critical assessment of their evening. The straight dope allows the restaurant to repair a shortcoming. "We can call customers back and ask them to return as our guests. We'd like to show them how sincere we are. We're not just here to take your money. If they come back we have made friends for life."

It isn't cheap putting the restaurant's money where its mouth is, says Trotter. "That's a practice almost unheard of—inviting people back and treating them to a couple-hundred-dollar meal. But it's all about the big picture. We work very hard at maintaining strong relationships with our guests. It's no big deal to extend gestures that demonstrate our sincerity."

SERVICE POINTS

To create a service system that is sensitive to customers' satisfaction levels and is relatively foolproof, consider these service points:

- Remain vigilant about your shortcomings; don't become enchanted with your accolades.

- Carefully examine situations that went wrong and devise ways to prevent them from occurring again.

- Apologize quickly for a mistake, even if you're not entirely responsible for it. An unhappy customer could badmouth your business.

- Create an additional layer or layers of service to backstop against mistakes. For example, make a manager available to pitch in during busy periods or when a complication arises.

- Overcome operational problems by redoubling teamwork.

- When serving customers, expect the "unbelievably unpredictable."

- Use a customer satisfaction survey to find out what you're doing right and wrong.

- Have both upper and middle management review customer satisfaction surveys and discuss with employees the ways to improve customer treatment.

- Have managers contact customers with a complaint and take remedial action—even if it has to come out of the bottom line.

- Use customer feedback to fine-tune your operation.

- Discuss letters of complaint and letters of praise at staff meetings.

- Treat a complaint as a gift; don't get defensive.

- Call customers to thank them for their especially glowing comments. Send them a gift as a token of your appreciation.

PART IV

EXCEEDING EXPECTATIONS:

ATTRACTING LIFELONG

CUSTOMERS

Want to make your customers friends for life? Then do something they'll never forget. Charlie Trotter's service team has compiled countless examples of things customers will long remember. Such gracious gestures extend well beyond the restaurant itself and into the charitable community, the neighborhood, and the restaurant industry.

9

Going the Extra Mile
(or Four) for the Customer

It's almost impossible to go above and beyond the call of duty at Charlie Trotter's because the service staff know their job is to do just about anything to satisfy a customer. Bending over backward for a customer is simply second nature to service staffers who think of themselves as concierges.

Although the guest had had the good sense to dine at Charlie Trotter's, he had made one big mistake. He left his car in the bank parking lot across the street.

The man who had made the 250-mile drive from Detroit discovered at the conclusion of his meal that his brown Acura wasn't where he had parked it. It was in the custody of the towing company whose phone number appeared on the bank's prominently displayed No Parking signs warning that violators will be towed.

He stomped back into the restaurant at 11:30 P.M. to report that his car had been towed. A receptionist lent a sympathetic ear and asked if she could call the auto pound for him. Reaching the towing company, the man demanded that they return his car to Trotter's. Fat chance, he was told.

Welcome to Chicago, where the towing companies don't do valet. Fortunately for the man with a bad case of indigestion there was Erwin Sandoval, the restaurant's expediter, who then spent the next ninety minutes expediting the recovery of the man's car.

ERWIN TO THE RESCUE

Rather than hail the man a cab to take him to the auto pound, which is in a neighborhood where many cabbies wouldn't want to go, Sandoval retrieved his own car and drove the guest to the dingy, dangerous-looking auto pound west of Chicago's Loop. As they pulled up in front of the auto pound, the man told Sandoval how much he appreciated the ride.

"He thought I was just going to drop him there," says Sandoval. "But I told him I was going to stay until he got his car." Good thing, because there was no one there when they arrived. Everyone was out towing cars. By the time someone from the company returned, it was nearly 1 A.M. The man paid the hefty towing fee and walked back to thank Sandoval for maintaining the late-night vigil for him before he drove off.

But that wasn't the last that was heard from the man. Several months later, Charlie Trotter received a letter expressing the man's gratitude to Sandoval and the restaurant for going the extra mile—actually about four—on his behalf. He promised to return, but in a cab.

AN INTUITIVE SENSE OF THOUGHTFULNESS

Charlie Trotter's had made another friend for life because a staff member went beyond the call of duty to help a guest. There are many tales of the service staff's heroic, thoughtful, or sincere gestures. They routinely and intuitively add a special touch to an evening by doing such things as tying a bow around a menu for souvenir purposes or giving Charlie Trotter baseball caps to young-sters dining with their parents.

Dan Fitzgerald spent a couple of hours one evening trying to return a cream-colored blazer to its rightful owner. As a guest was leaving one evening, she described her jacket to the staff at the front door. She thanked them for her coat, and she and her husband headed off into the night.

Along came another guest a half-hour later who requested her cream-colored blazer. She was a regular guest who came to Chicago several times a year from Ohio to dine at the restaurant and spend the weekend at the Drake Hotel. As she was handed a coat, she said it was not hers. Uh-oh. Fitzgerald, who was the assistant dining room manager at the time, realized the first woman was given the wrong blazer. He now had to find her and get the cream-colored blazers exchanged. In the meantime, the second woman returned to her hotel, sans blazer.

Fitzgerald checked the reservation list to see if the first couple had left a home number. But the guests were from out of town. For-tunately, they had confirmed their reservation from a limousine, and the number had been recorded in the reservation book. The num-ber was for the limo driver's cell phone. Fitzgerald reached the driver, who said he was parked outside a downtown nightclub where the couple planned to spend some time.

Fitzgerald and the limo driver then spent the next twenty-five minutes searching the dark and crowded nightclub for the woman. "Finally, I saw the blazer draped over the back of the woman's chair," says Fitzgerald. "I explained that she was given the wrong blazer, and I handed her the right one."

Next stop was the Drake Hotel, where Fitzgerald presented the woman from Ohio with her own cream-colored blazer. "Before I worked at Trotter's, I might have thought differently about how to resolve a situation like that, perhaps ship the right jackets to people rather than try to straighten a problem out immediately. But the longer you work here, the more innate those kinds of responses become."

When a guest leaves a coat or a briefcase or a purse behind, a service staff member will take a cab or drive to the person's home or hotel to return the item. The staff member often gets there before the guest does. Servers have called airlines to alert them that one of their passengers is running late. Could they please hold on for a few minutes?

TAKE MY TIE, PLEASE

Christian Giles has good taste in ties. His customers certainly think so. "One evening, a guest commented that I was wearing a beautiful tie, and we discussed where I had purchased it," says Giles. "I left the dining room, removed the tie, and put on another one. Then I wrapped the tie my guest liked in a box and offered it to him as a gift from Charlie Trotter's. He was stunned."

Giles says he's presented several of his gift-wrapped ties to guests. And so have his colleagues. "It's become a tradition for us at Charlie Trotter's. Whenever a guest comments on a tie, we wrap it up and present it to him or her with our compliments." But Giles's tie rack has not been depleted by his generosity. Guests have presented him gift-wrapped ties over the years. One good turn deserves another.

Service staff members have dashed out during service to buy greeting cards, disposable cameras, balloons, even six-packs of beer for their guests. "We had a guest in the other night who said he did not drink wine," said Francisco Estrada, a server assistant who works in the atrium-foyer bar. "He told me he drank beer, but only one kind: Corona. I told him we had a very limited beer selection. He wanted to know why we didn't have Corona." Rather than apologize, Estrada dashed out the door to the nearest liquor store and returned with a six-pack of the man's favorite beer. "He was extremely happy about it," says Estrada.

UP, UP, AND AWAY

The reservationists have added some special touches to a guest's evening. When making a reservation, a man said that he was treating his wife to dinner at Trotter's to celebrate her birthday and to announce that he was going to take her on a balloon ride the next day. Before the couple arrived for dinner, a reservationist went to a store and bought a bouquet of balloons, which was waiting for them that evening.

Trotter's has been the setting for countless marriage proposals—and not all of them accepted, staff members painfully reported. But the staff will do everything in their power to ensure all goes well on such a monumental evening. Gentlemen have occasionally entrusted engagement rings to servers, who will do a special presentation when it's time for the guest to pop the question.

"I've been there some evenings when his wife, Lynne, and his mother [Dona-Lee] are in the dining room. They were there to help the staff ensure that if guests so much as raised their eyes, their needs would be met. It's a wonderful environment. We've come to know everyone. It's more like a family dinner for us than a dining experience. It's very comfortable."

Michael Klein,
guitar company owner and former
manager of the Grateful Dead

On one occasion, a nervous young man called to make a reservation, and he explained that he planned to propose marriage over dinner. But he wanted to make the proposal memorably romantic. He wanted to couch his proposal in a poem, but he said he was no good at poetry. Could she help? The reservationist told him she was no poet either, but she'd give it a try. They worked out a poem over the phone, which the young man recited while extending the engagement ring. The proposal was accepted. Another satisfied customer.

The gestures needn't be grand whether it's at Trotter's or another service provider. For example, a stockbroker might include a newsletter in a client's monthly statement, a flight attendant might throw in an extra drink, a cataloguer might provide free delivery for a longtime customer, or a hotel could upgrade the room for a guest who'd endured a long day of travel delays.

I'LL BE YOUR CONCIERGE THIS EVENING

Veteran server Paul Larson says he enjoys going beyond his traditional role by acting as a sort of concierge for his guests. "We are often asked about our favorite restaurants or 'Where should we go for a quiet drink after dinner?' or 'Where can we go for jazz music?'" says Larson. "These are opportunities for you to evolve from your waiter role and become a concierge/liaison for your guest. Not only will I recommend a restaurant, but I will also interview the guests and ask them where they would like to eat dinner and 'Will just the two of you be dining?' in the event they may want to include additional guests."

He will then place a call to a restaurant for the guest, almost always securing a reservation. "Often, I can rely on a friend at that restaurant to provide the guests with extra special care. I only recommend restaurants where I have dined, unless additional advice comes from Charlie himself or another trusted associate."

Larson then presents a hand-addressed envelope that contains a hand-written message confirming the reservation. "The next time these guests happen to sit at my table, I will ask them how they enjoyed that dinner. However, they usually preempt my comment with their own thanks and compliments about their evening there."

Receptionist Makiko Hattori says people from out of town who have heard about Charlie Trotter's will walk in the front door during service and ask if they can get a table. The answer is almost always no because tables need to be reserved far in advance. Rather than just turn them away, Hattori will use the restaurant's considerable clout to reserve a table on short notice at another restaurant for walk-in visitors. She does all the legwork.

"One man who managed to get a reservation here the next night told me how thankful he was for my help and how much he enjoyed the restaurant where I got him a reservation," Hattori says.

TIPS FOR A COOL TIME

Jason Platt, a habitué of the city's jazz clubs, is often called upon to provide a recommendation for his guests looking for something to do after dinner at Trotter's. Both local and out-of-town guests seek his advice. His fellow servers often ask him for a tip on the best clubs to visit and then pass the recommendation along to their guests.

A growing number of guests request that the celebrity chef sign a Trotter cookbook they may have brought with them to dinner. Larson recalled an evening when a woman from out of town was dining at the restaurant. One of the purposes of her trip was to get Trotter to sign a copy of his book *Charlie Trotter Cooks at Home* for her mother to be presented as a Christmas gift.

But the woman forgot to pack her cookbook. "She was kind of upset and was planning to go buy another book and return the next day to get Charlie to sign it. I just went and got a copy of the book, asked Charlie to sign it for her, and presented it to her. She was amazed. Now she has a book for herself and a signed copy for her mother."

"GO AHEAD, MAKE MY DAY"

Server Rene Roman thrilled a customer when he arranged for a man and his wife to sit in on a taping of *The Kitchen Sessions* TV program. "The man was a chef at a small restaurant in Saskatchewan, Canada, and he had read all of the Trotter cookbooks. He was a big fan," says

Roman. "So naturally he was very excited about getting a cookbook signed by Charlie the evening he and his wife dined here. Unfortunately, Charlie was not available when they were here because a taping ran late into the evening, and Charlie had to go somewhere afterward."

Sensing the guest's disappointment, Rene sprang into action. He talked to Mitchell Schmieding, who went next door to the studio long enough to speak briefly to Trotter about the guest's request. On hearing the man was a fellow chef, Trotter told Schmieding to invite the man and his wife to sit in on the taping the next morning. "The man was so psyched when he heard what we were going to do for him. He loved every minute. It went way above his expectations."

Then there was the time when two out-of-town doctors who were in Chicago for a medical convention decided they wanted to have lunch at Trotter's. But the restaurant is dinner only. They tapped on the locked door of the restaurant. Trotter happened to answer the door and said he'd love to have them come for dinner some night. After thinking for a moment, Trotter invited them in. They followed him through the empty restaurant to the kitchen, where he quickly set up the famous table and cooked a multicourse lunch for them. They were delighted and none the poorer. Over their objections, Trotter would not give them a bill for their private feast he personally prepared for them.

After one regular guest gently complained on a Friday night that he could never land a reservation at the famous kitchen table where a meal is $175 a plate, Trotter asked the man and his wife to come back the next day at noon. "The table was all set for them. We prepared them a great meal. That's the mindset. Nobody can pay you enough money for what you do around here. It's not about the money. People feel good about working in an environment where these kinds of things are done for a guest."

GOING TO EXTREMES

Trotter's service team has been known to go the extra mile for customers in the most extreme conditions. Take the blizzard that roared out of the Rockies and across the Plains and blustered into Chicago on Saturday, January 2, 1999, piling up nearly two feet of snow. It was more than the city could handle. Power lines snapped, airports closed, trains stopped running, and motorists ditched their cars in the middle of the unplowed streets while the howling winds sculpted monstrous drifts.

But like the snow, the show went on at Charlie Trotter's—sort of. Employees knew that unless Trotter called them at home, the restaurant would be open. Twenty brave souls who trudged through knee-high, even waist-high, snow made it to the restaurant that day. One of the chefs was forced to abandon his car on a snow-clogged highway and walk several miles to the restaurant. A chef's gotta do what a chef's gotta do.

Trotter, who lives about a mile from the restaurant, was at the helm, determined to honor the reservations that guests had made long in advance of that wintry evening. But the evening's numbers were dwindling. Each time the phone rang, it was either a guest calling to cancel or an employee calling to report that he or she was snowbound. Some of the calls, however, were from guests calling to see if the restaurant would be open that evening. Come hell or high water, they said they would be there.

ORPHANS IN THE STORM

The first order of business was to dig out the restaurant. Several employees shoveled the front of the restaurant for the guests' access and the rear and side alleys to allow trucks to make food and supplies deliveries. Only a handful of trucks showed up. The wheels of commerce were nearly ground to a halt. Their digging was all but futile; no sooner had they shoveled the snow than the wintry gusts pushed it right back.

Nevertheless, nearly fifty guests, most of them from the neighborhood, drifted in that night. Some people from the neighborhood showed up at the door without a reservation figuring they would have a good chance of getting a table. They were right. "It was one of those nights when you do what you have to do," recalls one employee. "You can't throw people out of the restaurant who made such an effort just to get there. They all had a great time once they got here." The only out-of-town guests were a couple from Milwaukee, who, better late than never, made it to restaurant. But they wouldn't be able to stay long because they had to catch the last train to Milwaukee in two hours.

Trotter put them on a fast track. He seated them at the kitchen table and prepared them a sumptuous multicourse meal. They ate in about ninety minutes, less than half the time it takes a usual feast to unfold at that table. But these were desperate times. In the meantime, a server spent the next hour working the phones in search of a cab that could take the couple back downtown to Union Station. The taxi companies reported that their cabs either weren't running or were at least two hours behind. The server finally found a limousine company that would drive the couple to the train station.

"What's most remarkable is that Trotter's orchestra can perform at such a high level of perfection on a nightly basis. If people went there a hundred times, the staff could afford an occasional C-minus performance. But people don't go there a hundred times. They may only go once in a lifetime, and they can't be treated that one time to a mediocre performance."

Ray Harris, Wall Street financier who has eaten at Charlie Trotter's nearly 300 times

JAZZIN' IN THE KITCHEN

The menu that night was especially improvisational. Because most of the food deliveries didn't take place, the cooks were just winging it. They were cooking some cool stuff on a night when menus were abandoned. As the storm intensified, the heat went out in the north dining room. It was not an immediate problem, because two-thirds of the reservations had cancelled. The guests were moved to warmer climes in the restaurant.

A more serious challenge, however, would be getting some of the guests home. The few who made it to the restaurant in a cab from the Loop or an outlying neighborhood of the city weren't going to return that way. The cabs had vanished. The limos were long gone. The guests who mushed their way in a few hours earlier faced a treacherous trek home through stinging winds and mounting drifts.

Trotter sent a manager to his home around 9 P.M., where he dug out Trotter's jeep and threaded his way back to the restaurant. Over the course of the next two hours, the manager ferried guests through the snowy, silent streets of Chicago to their doorsteps.

LEAVE THE DRIVING TO US

The conditions were terrible and the jeep's pace was glacial, but Trotter's four-wheel drive vehicle rode out the storm. "People couldn't believe they were being taken home in Charlie Trotter's jeep," recalls the manager. "I don't think you would find many chef-owners who would have an employee go to his house, dig out his car, and drive guests to their home in the middle of a blizzard. That was one of our greatest nights of service."

Trotter's service team are accustomed to taking to the streets on behalf of customers. They'll routinely step out to flag down a cab for a departing guest. But that's not always easy. Just a few nights before the blizzard, the restaurant entertained two full seatings on New

Year's Eve in dining rooms festively decorated by the staff. "But as the night began to wind down, we realized we had a problem," recalls Christian Giles. "Taxicabs were difficult to find during the evening of celebration. By 2 A.M., approximately ten guests waited for rides to their destinations.

"So employees with cars volunteered their services by driving these guests to their hotels," says Giles, who drove two separate groups of guests to their hotels downtown, about four miles away. "They were extremely appreciative, and they couldn't believe we would use our own vehicles to escort them. But that's the way we do things at Charlie Trotter's. By the time I returned to the restaurant it was 4 A.M., and I still had two hours of work to perform."

WILD IN THE STREETS

Cabs were just as hard to come by on nights in the 1990s when Michael Jordan and the Chicago Bulls won the clinching games of the NBA championship. Revelers were everywhere on those nights and so were hooligans. Fearing for their own safety, cabbies made themselves scarce once the celebrations erupted in the street. Guests who had arrived in a cab probably weren't going to return to their homes or their hotels in a cab. "The city is up in arms on nights like that, and you can't find a cab anywhere," says Trotter. "So we would get our own cars and drive guests through all the drunken revelry and get them home. That's what it's all about." Everyone made it home in one piece and appreciative of the extra measure of service.

"Certainly the guests are pleased, but we don't do it for an ulterior motive," he says. "We do it because that's what we would want to experience if we were in the same position. Service people don't even need to ask permission. They just know that these are the kinds of things we do here."

PLAYING AN
EXTRAORDINARY ROLE

Another element that goes beyond the ordinary at Charlie Trotter's is the wine service, which is done with a unique flair at the restaurant.

"In a lot of restaurants, the bottles are opened out of sight at a serving credenza in the back of the dining room. But the beauty of the wine service is lost," explains sommelier Belinda Chang. But Trotter's serving credenzas are purposely placed in the middle of the dining rooms where guests can watch Chang and other members of the service team open and decant the wine. "It's a huge show. I'll notice every person in the dining room watching the beautiful decanting process. I'll hold a gorgeous crystal decanter up for everyone to see. It's all part of the entertainment here."

"The wine list offers plenty to plunder, including such fascinating offbeat selections as sparkling wine from Mas de Daumas Gassac or a dozen hot new wines from Australia. No weak choices clog this list, which is strong in areas that work well with food: Alsatian, German, Rhone in red and white, Burgundy in good vintages. Red Bordeaux shows some depth (17 vintages of Mouton-Rothschild back to '28)."

Wine Spectator

Wine is serious business at Trotter's, where Chang and the service team guide guests through the vast array of wine selections. Wine is a vital element with every dish, as either an ingredient or an accompaniment. For more than half of its fourteen-year existence, Charlie Trotter's wine program has been under the direction of Larry Stone and Joseph Spellman, the only two Americans ever to have won the world sommelier competition.

Chang was promoted to the prestigious position of sommelier at the restaurant in 2000 and is acutely aware of the restaurant's rich tradition in wine service. "This restaurant has an incredible legacy with wine service," says Chang, who has been certified by the Court of the Master Sommeliers. She is studying to take a series of exams that, she hopes, will lead to her designation as a Master Sommelier. Only thirty-two sommeliers in the United States hold that distinction.

THE CHEMISTRY OF WINE

A biochemistry major at Rice University, Chang says her chemistry classes have proved helpful at Trotter's and in preparation for the Master Sommelier exams because they gave her insight into the fermentation process.

But she's often called upon to be more of a historian than a scientist as the sommelier at Trotter's. "I will initiate a story about the wine as I'm presenting it and pouring it for guests. I might ask the guests if they have ever visited the winery or if they have met the owner. If they haven't, I will tell them more about it. People enjoy the stories about the various producers and vintages."

Chang says there is more presentation to the wine service at Trotter's than there is at restaurants that employ a wine steward whose role is to simply take the order, deliver it to the table, and open it. "We try to bring more depth of knowledge to the process," says Chang. "Even if people aren't ordering a particular wine, they may want to hear about it while they are here. They might ask if I have had it before. Or why it costs $10,000 a bottle. Or what makes it so special. People like to have that kind of discourse with a sommelier."

Guests in the restaurant for a business engagement are generally less receptive to a discussion about a wine's origins than those dining for more social purposes. Just as she did when she was a server, Chang attempts to carefully read the guest's needs and interest in wine. If the guest appears to be interested in a conversation about wine, she will enthusiastically discuss how a particular vintage compares to the last vintage or where one producer falls along the quality spectrum.

DISARM WITH CHARM

For some diners, especially first-time guests at Trotter's, the wine component of the dining experience can be the most discomfiting. Chang attempts to defuse such anxiety "by being there at the right moment. If I see someone quickly close the list out of frustration and say they have no idea what they want, I will step in and try to coax them through it. There is a huge intimidation factor." Extraordinarily friendly, Chang says she will begin to gently probe a guest's likes and dislikes as she poses such questions as: "What do you usually enjoy?" or "What producers are you familiar with?" Chang says it's important to be comforting to people who are unnerved by the wine decision as it could weigh on their entire dining experience.

Wine knowledge, she says, is "all about what you have tasted because you have to translate it to the guest." Chang tastes nearly every bottle that is opened in the restaurant to protect guests from defects, including a fungus that can infect the bottle's cork. "For example, the guest may have never tasted a certain California cabernet, but I have had it five times. I can tell if the bottle is off. I'm protecting the reputation of the winery as well as the guest from a bottle that might have a problem. I do it in full view of the guest at a serving credenza in the middle of the dining room." Chang says she gets questions all the time from guests as to why she does that. "Some people think it's very strange or some will laughingly say, "'No wonder you are so cheerful.'"

As sommelier, Chang is responsible for training the service staff and her assistant, Jason Smith, on wine service and wine knowledge. Each member of the service team is given the eight hundred-page *New Sotheby's Wine Encyclopedia.* It's not a gift. Servers are expected to study the chapters that pertain to the restaurant's list and acquire an almost encyclopedic grasp of wine. They are often called upon to assist with wine service and to conduct tours of the wine cellars. During weekly training sessions, Chang might have the servers focus strictly on champagne or on the glassware in which the wine is served.

Guests will invariably ask to be shown the most expensive bottle in the cellar and ask what makes it so expensive, says Chang. The biggest prize in the $1 million, 25,000-bottle collection is an 1870 Lafite.

BIG FUN DOWN UNDER

Another highlight for guests at the restaurant, particularly wine connoisseurs, is the opening of a large format bottle such as a Balthazar, a twelve-liter bottle of champagne. Specially made champagne tongs are used to carefully uncork the bottle, which, if done right, will barely make a sound, says Chang. "It's really spectacular to watch a Balthazar or a large-format red decanted and paraded around the dining room because they are so rare; perhaps only twenty to fifty of them have been made in a year. It's very special to drink from one of them," says Chang. "The chef [Trotter] likes to open the large bottles when we have a big event."

Wine collectors or people who have or plan to build their own wine cellars are particularly energized by a tour of the cellars, says Chang. "There are so many great restaurants in the United States that would never volunteer to show off their cellars because they are messy or not pristine. We love to show ours. They are definitely show cellars," says Chang. Nothing is off limits at Trotter's, where the restaurant's four cellars are meticulously maintained and carefully organized.

Two redwood cellars in the basement are dimly lit to protect the wine. Temperature and humidity are carefully set for the same reason. In the red wine cellar, for example, the temperature is a constant 58 degrees and the humidity is set to a range of 65 to 70 percent.

"People are impressed by how we divide the collection into climates," says Chang. "For example, the Alsatian, German, and Austrian wines with higher acid content need to be kept about ten degrees cooler than other whites downstairs. Those wines with higher acid content are stored in a cellar on the restaurant's second floor. A cellar in the studio kitchen primarily stores large format bottles, mostly reds."

A LIST TO BEHOLD

It isn't necessary to visit the cellars to be impressed with the restaurant's wine program, says Chang. "There's a very strong interest in wine among our guests. I'd say that at least half the people are here because they know we have an incredible wine list. They have either looked at it on the restaurant's Web site or they have read about it in a news article. They are so excited when we present it to them. Some will stare at the list. It's a huge part of the experience here."

Once or twice an evening, guests will ask to take an empty bottle home with them as a souvenir. "What they really want is the label, so I'll remove it for them and bring it to their table before they leave," says Chang.

LOVE AND MARRIAGE

Under Chang's stewardship, the wine list continues to evolve, with new selections added or old ones subtracted every two weeks. "We give a lot of thought to how well the wines work with food. They are not just cult wines. They all have a purpose. What we like to show on the list are food-friendly wines. Many of those come from the Burgundy and Bordeaux regions, both red and white."

Chang and the service team work carefully with a table to ensure that there is a happy marriage between the food and the wine. "The menu is designed so the first few courses are more delicate and white wine friendly," she explains. "In the second half of the menu, we typically move on to a richer, more red wine style of presentation."

But what if a guest is particularly partial to white wine or, conversely, red wine? No problem, says Chang. She will speak to the kitchen about adjusting a course to make it more compatible with that style of wine. "Let's say a table was about to receive a rich rabbit course with red wine reduction and foie gras, but the guests might say they weren't quite ready to move into red wine. They wanted another bottle of white. At that point, a server or I would run back to the kitchen and instruct them to do the rabbit course with a fava bean puree to make it more white wine friendly. We're essentially adding a course to ensure that what they are drinking pairs up with what they are eating."

ON SECOND THOUGHT

Guests are very grateful that "we can make those kinds of adjustments for them. It's all about being considerate of the guest. We're always willing to rethink a presentation," she says. Chang will sometimes try to subtly talk a guest out of a choice of wine if it blatantly clashes with a

"Dining at Charlie Trotter's is more than intricate cuisine and incredible wines. Service is the third key component of the 'Trotter's Experience.' Gracious, knowledgeable and friendly staff greet guests as they enter the door, guiding them through the degustation menus and wine selections as well as helping with any special requests. The exceptional wine cellar covers over 13,000 different selections to enhance your discovery of one of the brightest stars in gastronomy."

Rave Reviews

dish. "As the flavors progress, we want the wines to progress with them. I admit that I nudge people," she says. Guidance is especially important for a guest who has not given much thought to a wine selection or for a guest who's never dined before at a restaurant where the wine is so inextricably linked to the food.

"Sometimes people will tell me that all they drink is red wine, but I will suggest they at least try a splash of white to go with the more delicate first two courses. I will tell them that the red wine they have chosen might overwhelm the dish. In most cases, they say 'That sounds like a great idea. What do you recommend?'"

If the guest persists on drinking red with the initial courses, Chang will offer to have the chef adjust his or her menu to make the first two courses richer and more red wine friendly. "We will use the same foodstuffs, but we'll just make the flavors a little more powerful so the dish will work better with what the guest has chosen to drink. That's one of the really cool things we do here. Not many restaurants will automatically make those adjustments for a guest."

IN TROTTER'S WE TRUST

Another option is to tell the guest to forgo the menu. "Tell us what you like, and we'll just cook for you," are Chang's instructions to the guest. "You know our reputation or perhaps you've been here before. We'll take care of everything."

There are times when a guest will simply give Chang a wine budget for the evening's wine selections, be it $500, $1,000, or more. One evening, a couple who had dined eight times before at the restaurant and who were building a home in the neighborhood said they would like to be presented the option of three red wines. Cost was not a particular issue, they told her. Chang recommended three: one for $500, another for $850, and yet another for $3,000. The couple selected a $3,000 Bordeaux. Chang next visited the kitchen, where the chefs then built a series of courses around the expensive wine.

Guests occasionally do a double take when she explains that she is the restaurant's sommelier. Not only is she young, but she is a woman, and women have traditionally been relegated to secondary status in the male-oriented world of fine wine and haute cuisine. But those who question her qualifications because of her youth and gender have not daunted Chang.

"Some people are expecting someone older and wonder how knowledgeable I can possibly be. It's all about being armed with information. With training and knowledge, I can crush them with everything I know."

Spoken like a true master.

SERVICE POINTS

To create a service staff whose mission is to exceed the expectations of its customers, consider these service points:

- Create a lasting impression and build a bond with a customer through value-added tokens of appreciation.

- Encourage employees to think of themselves as concierges working on behalf of customers. At Trotter's, for example, the service staff don't just give customers a recommendation on a restaurant, they make the reservation for them.

- Bend the rules to create an unforgettable experience for each customer—even nonpaying customers.

- Welcome all customers, even in extreme circumstances. For example, Trotter's, with less than half its staff and a shortage of supplies and foodstuffs, put on a splendid evening for its guests on the night of a blizzard.

- Make your business as accessible as possible to customers. No part of Trotter's is off limits to guests.

- Educate employees about your business so they are competent and comfortable when dealing with customers.

- Challenge guests to try something new in your product or service mix.

- Be willing to customize an order on short notice.

- Use a touch of flair to present a company's strong suit. For example, the service team makes much ado about the opening of a large-format wine bottle.

10

Travels with Charlie

When a business takes to the road or extends its brand into a new venue, it should deploy the same principles and best practices that it uses at its primary operation. A "Trotterite" knows to uphold the organization's high standards regardless of the location.

Foodstuffs. Check. Bottles of Bordeaux. Check. Wine cradles. Check. Stemware. Check. Linens. Check. China. Check. Now packed and ready, Charlie Trotter is taking the show on the road. Regardless of where Trotter and his service team go, they always pack the same high standards that epitomize the restaurant.

Like a hospital that opens an off-site clinic or a brokerage firm that launches branch offices, Trotter's maintains its brand of service at off-site venues. Customers have the same expectations regardless of locale.

When Trotter's stages one of its out-of-house events, the restaurant's kitchen and dining room are virtually re-created—complete with elaborate bouquets. It could be in a private home or in a more institutional setting like a corporate boardroom or the James Beard

House in New York City, which Trotter has called the "Carnegie Hall of Culinary Arts." Ad hoc teams of service staffers and chefs have been dispatched just about everywhere—Toronto, California's Napa Valley, Philadelphia, and various locations in Chicago. The teams vary in size. Often they outnumber the guests at a private event.

HITTING THE JACKPOT

Trotter and his team will prepare the restaurant's trademark multi-course feasts that unfold over the course of three to four hours. Trotter doesn't charge the host a dime. The host has won the services of Trotter and his team through a charity auction. The winning bid is usually about $25,000, and it's the charity's to keep. Trotter's does about six to eight such dinners a year, on Sundays or Mondays when the restaurant is normally closed.

Senior Server Paul Larson has gone on many of the road trips during his eleven years at the restaurant. The events are not only a great way to see the country, he says, but they give the staff an inside look at people's tastes in living. "They're always very excited to have us in their home for a day," says Larson.

Like a SWAT team, the Trotter squad packs and carts off its coolers of food and boxes of supplies with great dispatch. "We've got the packing down to a science," he says. "Some of the food is prepped here, but the meal is cooked at the host site." What they can't control, however, are the inevitable weather delays and less explicable complications at Chicago's O'Hare International Airport.

"We've cut it close a couple of times when we've had problems at O'Hare," says Larson. And they've cut it close on return trips after a Monday night event. "We have flown back on Tuesday mornings and made it back just in time for service. We hit the ground running."

ON THE ROAD AGAIN

There is no diminution of the Trotter standards when working out of house. Mary Hegeman, an assistant to Trotter, has accompanied him on the road, helping with a variety of matters including handling media inquiries. Hegeman, who worked for a public relations firm before joining Trotter's, says Trotter employees know that regardless if they're in the restaurant or working an out-of-house event two thousand miles away, they still need to uphold the same standards.

Service on the road may be even better than at the restaurant because of the higher ratio of staffers to guests, says Larson. Even though there's no additional compensation for working a day on a weekend, Trotter has no problem finding volunteers to staff the events. Working a charity dinner is not only good for the soul, it's a chance to explore a new city if time permits. Trotter typically announces an event at a preservice meeting and invites people to see him afterward. Sometimes, he will draft a staff member for the event.

Often the guests at a private event in a home are friends of the restaurant. It's fun to see them in a different setting, says Larson.

GUESS WHO'S COMING TO DINNER?

Erwin Sandoval was part of a team that went to the Lake Forest, Illinois, home of a couple who successfully bid $25,000 at a Literacy Chicago charity auction. Sandoval, five other service staffers, eight chefs, and Trotter rendezvoused at the restaurant at 2 P.M. on a Sunday, packed the food and supplies, and motored up the North Shore to Lake Forest. A little over an hour later, the team had taken over the couple's home.

The eight chefs worked elbow to elbow under Trotter's watchful gaze, preparing the evening's grand menu for sixteen guests. The service team swept into the dining room, lending it the Trotter

"Trotter expects his staff to be as committed as he is. 'I look for people who are psyched and ready to do whatever it takes. Attitude is about being on fire—you approach work like it's a religious experience.' The three most important qualities he looks for, he says, are 'attitude, attitude, attitude.'"

The Scotsman

touch with the restaurant's silver, china, linens, and glassware. Floral displays were put in place.

Guests arrived at 6 P.M. as Sandoval and the servers took their coats and escorted them into the dining room, where Trotter greeted them. He described many of the courses, and sommelier Belinda Chang provided a wealth of colorful details about the wines she was serving that night. By 10 P.M., guests were leaving for home raving about the special evening prepared by America's best chef.

DIFFERENT VENUE, SAME SERVICE

Sari Zernich, who works in the restaurant's corporate office, says Trotter's does about sixty to seventy out-of-house events a year all over the country. In addition to the private dinners, events include Trotter's book signings and cooking demonstrations. Just as it does in the dining room, service comes into play at those events as well, says Zernich.

"The recipes at the demonstrations are often very spontaneous," says Zernich. "People will sometimes request the recipe even though Charlie has just created it." Nevertheless, she will retrace Trotter's steps, compile the recipe, and mail it to the person's home. If people can't find the ingredients for the dish, Zernich will head down to the kitchen to see if they have them in stock. If the person lives in Chicago, she'll invite the person to drop by the restaurant, where she'll give them a pound of hard-to-find mushrooms, for example.

She rarely charges for the ingredients. On other occasions, Zernich will send a person requesting a recipe or recipes one of Trotter's cookbooks.

She fields recipe calls throughout the year from people who have eaten at the restaurant and want to re-create the dish on their own. Sometimes she can point to a recipe in one of Trotter's cookbooks. Other times, she will have to write the recipe from scratch. She usually recommends ingredients that are readily available in a grocery store.

THE SECRET OF THE CHOCOLATE BLACK SHEPHERD'S PIE

Zernich also helps out people who were intrigued by a recipe Trotter used on his TV program. She has even handled phone calls and e-mails from people who have had meals at other restaurants and wanted advice on how to prepare them. Like the chocolate black shepherd's pie that a caller just had to have the recipe for. She explained that Trotter's doesn't do such a pie, but she'd be happy to walk the caller through the steps to create one. The caller explained that the restaurant that served the dessert refused to share the recipe with her. Its recipe for chocolate black shepherd's pie was apparently top secret.

Zernich says she's always willing to help. And who knows, the next restaurant that caller might visit could be Trotter's, where there are no secret recipes.

Zernich, who accompanies Trotter on many of the out-of-house events, says she can't help but notice the difference in approach to service between the Trotter employees and the employees at bookstores, museums, hotels, or others restaurants where the events have taken place. She recalled a recent cooking demonstration done in a tent set up outside a Chicago museum. While Trotter was demonstrating the preparation of a dish, a gust of wind toppled wine glasses and blew napkins off the guests' tables. Museum staff members didn't lift a finger to help. Not their department. Zernich, who was behind the stage, saw what happened and rushed to assist the guests.

THANKS FOR EVERYTHING

Zernich lent a hand one evening to an elderly woman who bought ten of Trotter's cookbooks at a Chicago bookstore where Trotter was signing copies. Zernich, who was assisting Trotter, saw a clerk bag the books for the woman at the checkout counter. As the woman struggled toward the door with the heavy bag of books, there was no offer of help from the staff, despite her age, much less the fact she had just bought nearly $500 worth of merchandise from them. Not their department. Zernich abandoned Trotter, unburdened the woman of the heavy bag of books, and walked her and the newly purchased books to her car.

Zernich isn't trying to sound self-righteous or heroic. What she did for those people at the museum or the woman at the bookstore was standard operating procedure. Her actions wouldn't even merit a pat on the back at Trotter's. "Working here you are so much more aware of the details. You are always watching and listening and making sure that whatever needs to be done for a customer will get done. After working here, paying attention to every detail makes perfect sense to me. I wouldn't think of doing it any other way."

She says the message of service truly sank in one evening when she was assisting Trotter at a charity dinner. Trotter and a group of chefs from various restaurants were preparing a six-course meal. It was learned that one of the guests was vegetarian, who asked if his menu could be modified. Some of the chefs complained that it would take too long to prepare a special meal for the guest. Another chef offered to remove any meat or fish from the guest's plate.

Trotter had heard enough. He stepped forward and said, "We got it!" Just because someone is vegetarian doesn't mean they shouldn't have a great meal, says Zernich. Trotter then prepared the guest a special six-course vegetarian meal. "I realized how different the standards are at our restaurant."

LOOK WHO'S MINDING THE STORE

The same standards are now being applied at Trotter's first foray into storefront retailing called Trotter's To Go.

The 3,300-square-foot storefront, which shares a nondescript commercial strip with a dry cleaner and a pack-mail store, opened amid a blizzard in December 2000. The store, about a mile from the restaurant, offers take-out food prepared fresh each day on the premises. Like the cuisine at the restaurant, the store features high-quality seasonal foodstuffs with an emphasis on organically raised products. The store carries a selection of sauces, artisan pastas, handmade chocolates, and specialty cooking equipment. More than 3,600 bottles of wine, organized not by region but by style, line some of the store's walls.

"A visit to Trotter's is like walking into the home of a good friend. It's a relaxed, friendly environment. I immediately find myself on a higher plane."

Ray Harris, Wall Street financier who has eaten at Charlie Trotter's nearly 300 times

Can a famous restaurateur make it as a neighborhood shop owner? Trotter sure thinks so. Running a restaurant and running a storefront take-out are "almost identical. You don't have tables and silverware, but everything else is the same." He's extended his service doctrine to the street, where customers are treated like guests in his restaurant.

"It's about doing things for guests before they have a chance to ask for something," says Trotter. "It's escorting people back to their cars with their bags. It's greeting people with smiling, sincere friendliness." The style of service in the store springs from the same put-yourself-in-the-shoes-of-the-customer philosophy that underlies service in the restaurant, he says. "The model is the model in my head, which says this is the way I would like to be treated if I walked into a neighborhood store, and these are the things that I would like to find there."

Trotter describes the store as a work in progress. "Our strength is that we don't exactly know what we are doing. We're not beholden to a certain retailing formula that says certain products have to be displayed on shelves at eye-level or that certain products have to be at certain price points or that labor costs have to be at a particular level. We are willing to reinvent how it all can be done, and we never imagine that something can't be done. It seems like a pretty good way to do it."

Just as he does at the restaurant, Trotter focuses on the store's top line rather than the bottom line. He tends to buy the best equipment and hire and train the best people. "Pursuing excellence in service and product and not compromising on that front will ultimately take care of the bottom line."

TROTTERIZING THE NEW TEAM

A key challenge is instilling the Trotter service philosophy in a group of twenty new employees. A handful of the store's employees are former Trotter employees who returned to the fold to assist with the launch. They have helped to inculcate the new hires with the intensely customer-focused attitude of a card-carrying "Trotterite." The new hires were given a taste of Trotter-style service one evening before the store opened. They were invited to the restaurant's studio kitchen dining room, where they were pampered by the wait staff, who served a traditional degustation menu over the course of three hours.

The store employees were mightily impressed by the dining experience, but they were also a bit daunted by the level of service that was lavished upon them by the wait staff of their sister business. Eric Werner, the store's assistant manager, did not work previously at the restaurant. But he's come to know the restaurant's high standards and the equally high standards that are expected at the store. He listens carefully to tales of service from the Trotterites assigned to the store, who often point out how much slower the pace is at the store than at the restaurant, which at any given moment can have seventy-five guests who need attention. Werner and his fellow store employees have become familiar with Trotter, who is frequently at the store. They must be ever-vigilant as the store is less than two blocks from Trotter's home.

"As a guest at the restaurant, I was made to feel like I was the only person in the dining room," says Werner. "It's as if everyone is focused on you. And that's what we want to do here. Dinner at the restaurant gave me an appreciation for how much care and love go into the food. Again, that's something we need to do here but on a different scale."

SMALL-TOWN TOUCH IN THE BIG CITY

Werner, who grew up in a town of two thousand in upstate New York, says he wants to re-create a sense of small-town intimacy in the store by coming to know the customers' tastes. Most of the store's customers hail from the surrounding neighborhood. Recognizing returning customers, just like in the restaurant, is critical to creating an environment where they feel that the staff values them, says Werner. He says it's especially rewarding to see a customer return to the store on a regular basis.

Some of the customers, particularly first-time guests, are almost taken aback by how they are treated by the staff, who are quick to offer customers a free taste of the food. Werner says people aren't sure how to react when the staff offer to help them out to their car with a bag. Some suspect that they're being hustled for a tip, which is not the case. "It's just a different approach to service," says Werner, who believes that most shoppers are conditioned to indifferent treatment.

BEYOND THE CALL OF DUTY

Kurt Sorensen, the store's general manager, says he makes it clear to the staff "that you're not just here to chop onions or make sandwiches." Their mission is much broader than that. He wants the staff to treat customers the same way he treated guests at the restaurant for many years.

Any one of the store's employees, whether they're working the counters or the floor in the front or preparing food in the kitchen, will interact with customers. Chefs proudly provide backstage tours of their gleaming kitchen and its sparkling top-shelf equipment. A large display window gives customers a front-row view of activity in the pastry station, where pastry chef Michele Gayer says she's always tweaking the offerings to appease the customers' sweet tooths. Anything goes for the customer.

"While the physical appearance of Charlie Trotter's has changed over the years, its philosophy of seamless service has not. There is never a sense of struggle to the service. It has always had a gracious feel to it. They are incredibly thoughtful. It begins with the moment you make your reservation and lasts until the moment they're walking you to the door at the end of the evening."

Charles Sitzes, a Chicagoan who has been dining at the restaurant since its earliest days

"One of the cooks in his chef whites was out on the street try-ing to a hail a cab for a couple that told him their next stop was O'Hare Airport," says Sorensen. "He knew just what to do. The Trotter mindset is all encompassing. It's how you graciously open the door for a customer, to how carefully you sweep the floor or how expeditiously you help a guest locate a hard-to-find product. We don't want to say 'no' to people. Anything within our reach, we'll reach for it."

In the same egalitarian spirit as the restaurant, Sorensen says every customer gets treated with an equal level of care. "We have some celebrities who come to the store, but we treat them the same way we would anyone else. Everyone is of equal importance to us."

REFINING SERVICE IN THE STOREFRONT

There are subtle distinctions between the kind of service practiced at Trotter's To Go and that practiced by the traditional food retailer. "We work on how we address the guests," says Sorensen. "Rather than say: 'Do you want something?' when a guest walks up to the counter, we'll say 'Do you care for a taste?' Just like in the restau-rant, we think there is a gentler, more refined way of doing things."

While the Trotter's To Go name suggests food on the run, Sorensen says customers tend to linger in the store and marvel over all the merchandise and the foodstuffs. Culinary students are par-ticularly fascinated by all the store has to offer and often will carefully study every ingredient. The customers' lengthier stays allow the staff to begin establishing relationships with them, says Sorensen.

In addition to a handful of Trotterites, the store's staff includes culinary students, students from nearby DePaul University, and peo-ple from the neighborhood with an interest in food and wine. A half dozen of the early hires who could not maintain the brisk pace and adopt the Trotter service style were dismissed.

MASS APPEAL

While the food at the store is consistent with the restaurant's culinary philosophy of high-quality seasonal foodstuffs, the food is not the restaurant's food to go. And it's certainly not in the same price range as that of the restaurant, where a guest pays $110 for the centerpiece of an entire dining package. The store's prices are very street level. Soups begin at $3.95, sandwiches at $5.95, and desserts at $1.25. It's great food for the masses.

Mark Signorio, Trotter's special projects director, says the store does not want to be perceived as a gourmet shop where the food and merchandise are often expensive. He believes the store, which he designed, has price points as affordable as the delis in the neighborhood grocery stores. They, of course, don't have the culinary cachet of the Trotter name. The shop also differentiates itself from grocery store delis with unique and hard-to-find specialty items such as organic soy sauces from Japan, special rices from China, equipment like truffle slicers or sharpening blocks and a selection of cookbooks that have been handpicked by Charlie Trotter.

The store is a feast for the senses. The walls are adorned with colorful paintings by artist Annette Turow, sweet scents from the pastry department mingle with the aroma of game roasting on a wood-burning spit rotisserie, and all is accompanied by cool jazz streaming from the store's speakers. A crimson canopy, mimicking the canopy on the restaurant's exterior, unifies the series of three storefronts that form the store.

Signorio says the store's audience is threefold: people who don't want to cook, serious home chefs, and wine aficionados who delight in the store's wine offerings. He believes the store's opening was well-timed to correspond with a period of more discriminating palates.

Wine shoppers are given a color-coded note card that offers stylistic descriptions of a particular wine style, which is supported by a listing of foodstuffs that complement that particular style of wine. The wine style called "Juicy, Fruity Reds" would be paired with foodstuffs such as Thai barbecue sauce, chanterelle mushrooms, black bean sauce, muscovy duck confit, or spit-roasted quail.

Trotter says the restaurant's well-established reputation was a huge asset in the store's successful launch. "Customers were coming through the door without even a sign or an address on it," he says. But starting the store was more than simply extending the brand. It proved just as challenging as starting the restaurant in 1987. "It's training a group of people and instilling a mindset so service to a guest becomes second nature. It's the idea of people giving of themselves 150 percent regardless of whether they are working twelve hours a day or four hours a day. It's the idea, whether you're in the restaurant or in the store, that no job is beneath them. Every task is of equal importance."

SERVICE POINTS

To apply a successful business's customer-service formula in a new venue, consider these service points:

- Observe the same standards and execute the same level of service regardless of your location.

- Remind employees that they play an ambassadorial role for the company when on the road.

- Ask employees to volunteer for company charity events; everyone feels great afterward.

- Encourage employees to offer assistance or helpful advice to anyone who needs it, even if that person is not a customer (yet).

- Extend the customer-focused approach to other aspects or divisions of a business.

- Delight new customers with an exceptional level of service.

- Don't be hidebound by a template when launching a new business.

- Have veteran employees inculcate new employees with your business's culture and values.

- Make it clear to all employees—even those backstage—that it's their job to interact with and help customers.

- Look for gentler, more refined ways to speak to customers.

11

Goodwill Hunting

A successful business says a lot about itself in how it treats its community's less fortunate, its neighbors, and its industry. With a pronounced humanitarian bent, Charlie Trotter and his restaurant pay scrupulous attention to all of those communities. Employees say it makes them feel good to work for a business with a soul.

"I hear you guys have a taste for exotic food like sea slugs and innards and things like that," Charlie Trotter said to the mortification of a group of fifteen inner-city high school students seated at the table in his studio kitchen. A bit intimidated by the serenity and elegance of the dining room, the students had yet to sense that Trotter had his tongue firmly planted in his cheek.

"And I have one very firm rule here," he deadpanned. "Not a single fleck of food can be left on your plate." The students' expressions grew even more desperate as Trotter's service staff tried to stifle a collective laugh. The father of a school-aged boy, Trotter knows the right buttons to push with kids who've been admonished all their lives to eat their vegetables. Yuck! But with a twinkle in his eye, he assured his racially diverse audience that he wasn't really going to subject them to anything as repulsive as sea slugs.

Yet the sumptuous meal he was about to serve them—fresh cod with black trumpet mushrooms, braised pork shoulder, Maine skate wing with watercress—struck them as nearly as exotic. This was no brownbag lunch. The students and three of their teachers were being treated to the same kind of multicourse tasting menu that would cost his regular guests $115 a plate. The one exception to the regular dining experience: the sommelier poured the students glasses of fruit juice. But do the math. This kind of charity isn't cheap.

CLEAN THE PLATE CLUB

There were no complaints about the food once three servers delivered the plates. "Man, this is great," cooed one student after sampling a bite of the braised pork shoulder. The plates were heading back to the kitchen with nary a scrap of food left on them. The truth be told, Trotter could very well have served the kids a Trotterized version of sea slug, perhaps gilded with truffles, and the students would have loved it too.

Two afternoons a week, yellow school buses park outside Charlie Trotter's as the students and several of their teachers are treated to a field trip to the world-renowned restaurant. It's part of Charlie Trotter's Culinary Education Foundation, a two-part philanthropic program that exposes students to fine dining and raises scholarship money for aspiring culinary students. A series of fund-raising dinners at the restaurant have generated more than $180,000 in recent years to pay for scholarships, explains Trotter. "The plan is to now raise $150,000 a year and give half away each year to scholarships, the remainder to go into a long-range fund that we hope will reach $1 million." Once the $1 million mark is achieved, the fund will provide an annual endowment for culinary school scholarships.

Trotter says giving back to the community is enormously rewarding for both for him and his staff. "Everyone gets a sense of fulfillment from the contributions we've been able to make to the community," says Trotter. "People feel good about working in an environment in which this kind of public service can happen."

Good works are their own reward, but they lift the spirits of employees and can be an important recruiting point for service providers of every stripe.

BEING A GOOD CITIZEN

One of the greatest rewards to running a successful, profitable business, says Trotter, is being in the position to write a check for a hospital or school, raise money for the arts, or mentor a young person. Trotter says he doesn't do it for PR value. The gestures speak for themselves.

The staff get a charge out of working with the kids on Wednesday and Thursday afternoons throughout the school year. Word of the program has spread far and wide throughout the city. Staff members give the youngsters special tours of the wine cellars, the ever-humming kitchen, and the studio kitchen where Trotter tapes his PBS cooking show. Trotter says the school program gives him and the staff the chance to interact with a much different kind of clientele or potential clientele, and it makes everyone more thoughtful about what they do.

"Charlie Trotter has set the highest standards in the industry and stretches them even farther. He sets his personal standards so high that he elevates the standards of everyone on the staff. No one wants to disappoint Charlie in his never-ending pursuit of excellence."

Michael Klein,
guitar company owner and former
manager of the Grateful Dead

"How has Trotter cooked up such acclaim? By creating a style of food—and designing a style of service—that sets him apart from even his most talented peers. His recipe for success holds lessons for everyone who's wrestling with how to stand out in an environment in which competition is tougher than ever, expectations are higher than ever, and the sacrifices for success are bigger than ever."

Fast Company

The school program has other goals. "It's also an opportunity to expose their palates to something other than pizza, hamburgers, and fries," says Trotter. "And it exposes students to a number of people who are genuinely enthusiastic and passionate about what they do. The program is not necessarily intended to get the students excited about the culinary arts."

PASSION ON PARADE

During the program, Trotter will introduce a handful of his employees. On this occasion chef de cuisine Matt Merges stepped into the studio kitchen dining room and served up a lesson on the importance of teamwork and a passion for everything you do. He explained how twenty-two people pull together each night in the kitchen to produce the restaurant's remarkable cuisine. "We're like a family. Sometimes we all don't get along so well, but we get the job done," said Merges, who told the kids that the first dish he ever made was egg salad. Today, he says his favorite dish is anything with fish in it.

Next up was morning sous chef Reggie Watkins, an African-American who, like some of the kids at the table that day, grew up in a tough Chicago neighborhood. Cheerful and gregarious, Watkins joined the restaurant in 1987, making him Trotter's most senior employee. He excitedly described his day and how he inspects every foodstuff from some of the world's top purveyors that comes through the door. Any item that doesn't meet Trotter's impossibly high standards gets sent back. "If you're passionate about what you do and always pursue excellence, I know you'll succeed." The kids seemed to hang on his every word.

A student asked if he had a life outside the kitchen. "I do. I have a great life and my greatest joy is my daughter, who is now in culinary school studying to be a chef."

Trotter asked Watkins: "Is it fun working here or what?" "Oh, yes," he replied. "We get to see food from all over the world. Wouldn't you say that's fun, chef?" Trotter naturally agreed, noting that "the more you learn around here, the more you realize all the things you don't know."

THE INQUISITION

Trotter wasn't quite done with the students. He was going to make them sing for their supper. "You now have to ask two questions of either me or the staff." Some of the students sunk into their seats, rattled by Trotter's request and fearing embarrassment. No questions were forthcoming, but Trotter would have none of that. "I mean it! Two questions from everyone."

The first question was: "What makes you happy?" Trotter shot back: "I'm not that interested in happiness. You can walk down the street and see something that makes you happy. I'm more interested in satisfaction, and you achieve that by setting goals, meeting them, and then setting new goals for yourself. I feel a sense of satisfaction when someone tells us that we have exceeded their expectations. That's the highest compliment you can receive."

The floodgates were open. The students realized it would be fun to pick Trotter's well-furnished brain. "How do motivate your employees?" "Not my job," he replied. "I don't believe in management. I don't have time for it. But I am very interested in leadership.

Don't rely on managers to set goals for you. You need to set goals for yourself. Your standards should be higher than your boss's."

"Where did you go to cooking school?" Trotter explained that he briefly went to culinary school after college, but he was largely self-taught thanks to a series of valuable apprenticeships. "I went to college at the University of Wisconsin and majored in political science and philosophy. I dropped out during my junior year because I regarded the undergraduate experience as an opportunity to read some great books. But I went back and got my degree. And I'm glad that I did."

"What was the most inspirational book you read?" Trotter pondered that one. "My greatest inspiration is the work of Dosteovsky, the Russian writer. He often said that young people must be willing to make a five-year sacrifice to set the stage for their careers. But not a lot of young people are willing to do that. It will pay off, however," Trotter assured the students.

THE RESTAURANT'S DEEP ROOTS OF CHARITY

Trotter's charitable efforts go back to the restaurant's earliest days when he began the Guest-Chef-for-a-Day program. People at charity auctions bid for the chance to spend a shift in the famous kitchen and watch Trotter and his team of chefs prepare the night's feast. Bids for a behind-the-scenes look at the operation sometimes top $2,000. Every night there's a guest chef who's put to work slicing, dicing, and helping prepare stock or assisting in other ways to produce the grand cuisine. Charitable organizations will also raffle off a Guest-Chef-for-a-Day certificate to raise money.

Visiting chefs from around the city, the country, and the world will ask to spend time in the Trotter kitchen to hone their craft with some of the best culinarians in the business. In exchange for the privilege, chefs are asked to donate $1,000 to a favorite Trotter charity for every week they spend in the kitchen.

Trotter has twice served as the chairman of the American Society's Vinaffair: Art of the Earth dinner and silent auction. In 1999, the event raised about $850,000, surpassing the organizers' goal. He has also raised money for the Make-a-Wish Foundation; Providence-St. Mel, an inner-city Catholic high school; Literacy Chicago; and such leading Chicago cultural institutions as the Lyric Opera, The Goodman Theater, and the Ravinia Music Festival.

COOKING FROM THE HEART

Trotter has raised hundreds of thousands of dollars for charities over the years by hosting cooking demonstrations either in his studio kitchen or off-site. Guests typically pay about $100 apiece to watch him prepare several dishes. And they get to sample his handiwork. The two-hour events are an opportunity to pepper Trotter with questions about cooking tips, recipes, and his cooking philosophy. Members of his service staff are always on hand to assist the guests with the food and wine.

One of the restaurant's most spectacular fund-raisers was done in conjunction with its tenth anniversary in August 1997. The seventy-five guests at the formal, invitation-only event paid $1,000 a plate to benefit one of Trotter's favorite charities, the Mercy Home for Boys and Girls on Chicago's hardscrabble West Side. Four youngsters from the home formed a receiving line at the restaurant's entrance to welcome the guests.

Roger Verge, the renowned chef from Moulin de Mougins near Cannes, and Angelo Gaya, a legendary Italian wine producer, flew to Chicago especially for the occasion. The evening's highlight was Trotter's presentation of a $75,000 check to Father James Close, Mercy Home's director.

LENDING YOUTH A HAND

Father Close told Trotter that evening about a young man who once lived in the home who aspired to be a chef. The young man, Aaron Lindgren, had attended culinary school and had worked in bakeries in Chicago and Colorado. Trotter asked Father Close to have the young man contact him. It wasn't long before Lindgren was put to work in Trotter's pastry department. After surviving the demanding environment at Trotter's, Lindgren went on to work in some of Chicago's top kitchens.

Trotter's public service ventures include guest speaking to business students at the University of Chicago and at Northwestern University. True to his spontaneous nature, Trotter doesn't prepare a lecture. He talks from his heart about the beauty and rewards of entrepreneurship, passion, motivation, leadership, public service, and, of course, his gospel of customer service.

He hammers home a central point about entrepreneurship to each class: "Don't do it for money. Do it for love because the money will take care of itself. Don't start a company because you believe it's the best industry in which to make a buck," he tells them.

"Start the business because you love the nature of that particular field or because you have a unique product. The greatest thing you can do is to start a business. You'll achieve great fulfillment if you go that route. And when your business is a success, you will be able to give back and enhance the community."

MISTER TROTTER'S NEIGHBORHOOD

Another community of great importance for Trotter and any business is the local neighborhood. Trotter tells his employees that their day doesn't begin when they walk in the restaurant's back door. It begins a few blocks away.

He encourages his staff to develop great respect for the neighborhood around the restaurant. The motorist they cut off for a parking spot on one of the side streets in the neighborhood, where parking is at a premium, may be the guest they wait on that evening. Trotter's admonition may be on the mark. A good percentage of the restaurant's guests come from Lincoln Park, a neighborhood of tree-lined streets and vintage townhouses and brownstones four miles northwest of Chicago's Loop.

"I suggest they pick up a discarded soda can in the gutter or litter on the sidewalks. It's a sign of respect for the neighborhood and community," says Trotter. He wants his staff to display the same kind of care for the neighborhood that they do for the guests. It's part of the thinking at the restaurant where no task is any less significant than another.

Employees meticulously maintain the sidewalk and the portion of the bustling street in front of the restaurant, sweeping and hosing down the pavement everyday. The restaurant valets arrive well before the guests to collect any stray litter in front of the restaurant. During a January snowfall, head valet Joe Vodak was seen brushing snow off cars—not just the cars of the restaurant's guests, but *every* car on the street for two blocks in either direction.

SPIT 'N' POLISH

Walk around to the back of the restaurant and behold the cleanest alley in Chicago. Trotter's crew has been there too, policing the alley for litter as well as sweeping and hosing off the pavement. In the winter, employees shovel snow from the alley and sidewalks. Trotter has been known to dispatch an entire crew of employees, none whose job can be described as street sweeper, to improve the alley's appearance. Neatness truly counts.

As another sign of respect for the neighborhood, Trotter eschews any garish signage on his restaurant. In fact, people unfamiliar with the restaurant might not even realize it was there. Some guests have complained that they were late for their reservation because neither they nor their cab driver, expecting a more commercial facade, could find Chicago's most celebrated restaurant.

In the late spring, summer, and fall, the restaurant is all but invisible behind a screen of concord grape vines and a row of flowers. Guests or passersby who look closely enough at the red-brick townhouse at 816 West Armitage Avenue will discover a small brass plaque indicating it's Charlie Trotter's. Just below it is a brass-rimmed window that displays the evening's menu. The restaurant planted four pear trees in the city-owned parkway between the sidewalk and street. Inlaid red bricks, paid for by the restaurant, further enhance the parkway's appearance. "To me, it's all about subtlety. I hate big signage and gaudiness," says Trotter, whose restaurant was influenced by New York City's tasteful looking brownstone restaurants that blend in with their surrounding neighborhood.

MY LOSS IS YOUR GAIN

Trotter's neighborliness has extended to the Greater Little Rock Baptist Church, one hundred feet west of the restaurant. (Trotter can cite the exact distance to the house of worship because if it were any closer to the restaurant, the city would not have granted Trotter's a liquor license.) If any of the restaurant's delicate Wedgwood china develops so much as a hairline crack, it becomes the property of the largely African-American congregation several doors away. "We have a great relationship with them," says Trotter. "They have one of the more extraordinary plate collections in the country."

Trotter began building a relationship with the neighborhood even before he opened the restaurant. "I wanted to let people know that we weren't going to be just another restaurant and bar," says Trotter. Nightlife is plentiful on the commercial strips in Lincoln Park, and neighbors are naturally wary of any new entrants. Little did they know what Trotter had cooking.

MEET THE NEIGHBORS

Although no one from the neighborhood protested his building permit or liquor license application, he launched a preemptive strike by knocking on doors of homes near the site of his restaurant. "I cooked several meals in the homes of the neighbors to show them that my restaurant was not going to be just more of the Lincoln Park bar/restaurant scene," says Trotter. "I wanted to reassure them. It wasn't that there was any resistance. I just didn't want it to become an issue."

The young entrepreneur, only twenty-seven years old at the time, also went door-to-door over the course of several city blocks to tell residents that if there was ever a problem with the restaurant's appearance or an employee or with the valet service, they should call him directly.

Trotter has since hosted dinners at the restaurant with all the trimmings for firefighters assigned to stations in the neighborhood. In more recent years, a staff member brought a meal each night to the nearby home of an elderly woman in poor health who lived alone. On holidays and special occasions, staff members were dispatched to her home to assist her to the restaurant where she would be given the royal treatment. The woman, who died in 2000, has never been a customer. Just a neighbor.

> "These are not busboys and waiters and runners tonight. They are True Believers, adepts on hand to escort the culinary pilgrims on their trip to the Holy Land. Because that is Charlie Trotter's mission, to arouse and inspire, to convert the uninitiated, to awaken the senses and rekindle the soul."
>
> Chicago *magazine*

MR. LARSON, I PRESUME

Whether they are in the restaurant or in the neighborhood, Trotter's service staff innately understand that they represent the restaurant, on duty or off. Senior server Paul Larson says it's important to dress and act appropriately because he's always running into guests of the restaurant. Because Trotter's is an international dining destination, it's possible to encounter a guest almost anywhere, including the airport in Brussels, Belgium.

While on vacation there, a woman approached Larson, who was wearing a hat and sunglasses at the time. She asked, "Do you work in the service industry?" Larson acknowledged that he did. "She then said, 'You work at Charlie Trotter's. You were our waiter. We had such a fantastic time.'"

Larson and the woman continued to compare notes while waiting for their respective flights. "She and her husband have since become regulars at the restaurant," says Larson. "The woman is a teacher at the Latin School [in Chicago], and she was invited by Charlie Trotter to bring her class to the restaurant. They had grown their own foodstuffs in a garden at the school and were asked to plan a menu around them. You never know how far relationships will snowball."

CLOSE ENCOUNTERS

Usually, says Larson, the encounters are closer to home. "On Sundays, a lot of waiters dine in restaurants because that's our day off. It's uncanny how often I'll see either a regular customer of Charlie Trotter's or an out-of-town guest who's making the rounds of the city's restaurants," he says. "While this may seem an awkward situation to some, it actually can evolve into a natural conversation with someone you know. I may ask: 'How was your day?' or 'What did you order on the menu tonight?'"

Larson says it helps to remember details of the evening when the guest was in the restaurant. "They are really touched by that," he says. Larson even plays an ambassadorial role with the various cabbies who drive him to work each day. Though not all of them could find the restaurant, they have all heard about it. "They are very curious about the restaurant. The five-minute cab ride gives me the opportunity to tell them about the restaurant in the best possible way," says Larson, noting that it's always helpful to educate a cabbie who might steer some business to the restaurant.

"I tell them that dinner at the restaurant is an incredible experience, it's a multicourse meal featuring seasonal foodstuffs. The menu changes constantly and, although it's expensive, it's an incredible value." What cabbie wouldn't be sold after an enthusiastic pitch like that?

Larson says, "No matter where you are, you can always run into a former or a future guest. Lesson learned? Always be proper, dress properly, and behave correctly. Be a perfect gentleman. Remember that your association with these people began at Charlie Trotter's."

IT'S A SMALL, SMALL WORLD

Sommelier Belinda Chang often runs into customers when she's away from the restaurant. Not surprisingly, she's crossed paths with customers a half dozen times at Sam's Wine & Liquors. Despite the pedestrian-sounding name, the store on the North Side of Chicago not far from Charlie Trotter's is considered the best wine retailer in the Midwest.

"I'll be looking at a bottle, and I'll notice someone kind of looking at me," says Chang. "Believing they recognize me, they'll approach and say: 'Aren't you Belinda, and don't you work at Charlie Trotter's?'"

Acknowledging that she's the friendly neighborhood sommelier, Chang's memory will often be put to the test in the aisles at

Sam's. "Do you remember the great white wine you chose for us? Can you help us find it?" the former guests may ask.

Odds are that Chang, who serves wine at hundreds of tables a month, won't recall the wine or its vintage, but she'll eagerly launch a search with the aid of a few clues. "I'll ask whether they remember what country or the year or just go through some possible options with them. I'm happy to take a few minutes to give them a hand." For Chang, it's just another day in Mr. Trotter's neighborhood.

MY FELLOW CULINARIANS

As important as the philanthropic community and the neighborhood is the nation's culinary community, which Charlie Trotter's has long served for both altruistic and commercial purposes.

On the commercial side, since 1997 Trotter's has been training and inspiring chefs and managers for Aramark, a Fortune 500 corporate food service giant with clients throughout the world. The Aramark consulting contract, along with the sale of Trotter's line of hot-selling cookbooks and other entrepreneurial ventures, provides the restaurant with additional revenue. "The ventures, in a sense, allow us to live beyond our means. We make good money at the restaurant but we spend whatever we make, and we don't want to get into debt," says Trotter.

He and his staff wrote a series of special menus that Aramark uses to provide a grander dining experience in their corporate dining rooms they use when hosting dinners and receptions. Throughout the year, Aramark managers and chefs from all over the world spend time at Trotter's learning the secrets of great service and extraordinary cuisine.

A FIVE-STAR IMPRESSION

"What were your impressions?" inquired Mitchell Schmieding of two visiting Aramark managers from Glasgow, Scotland, who spent the previous day at the restaurant. Seated in the balcony dining room the next morning, the Aramark chef said he was impressed.

"It is unique the way you pull things together. Your reservation system is very efficient. You know that a guest has a birthday. That's good marketing. The restaurant is run like a five-star hotel," he said. "I like the idea of you bringing customers into the kitchen. At most restaurants you couldn't do that because there would be swearing and tantrums. Perhaps it's the presence of guests that helps control that kind of behavior. I also noticed that there does not appear to be a battle between the front of the house and the back of the house. It seems to gel here because both units work as a team."

The level of communication between the service staff and the guests impressed him as well. "You are always communicating with the guest. Everybody is very professional about it. It starts at the front door and goes right to the back." He was also taken with the business suits the servers wore. In class-conscious Great Britain, he observed, servers in fine dining restaurants wear uniforms to signify their working-class status while the guests wear suits. "Your attire is equal to that of your customers. I wish we could do that in Great Britain."

OPERATING WITH A CONTROLLED FURY

He characterized the pace in both the dining room and the kitchen "as a controlled fury. There is a sense of immediacy, but not a sense of panic," which he noted customers will quickly detect and make them feel uncomfortable. Schmieding explained that the front of the house and the back of the house work well together in the heat of battle because there are clearly delineated rules of the road.

KNOW THY PRODUCT

The Aramark managers, who sat in on the previous evening's pre-service meeting, were surprised that it was the servers, not the chefs, who described the food that was going to be presented that evening. And they were equally surprised to see chefs in the dining room describing courses to guests. Based on their experiences in Europe, it would be unusual for a chef to leave the kitchen and describe a dish in the dining room. Schmieding explained that every employee needs to have a working knowledge of each other's position at the restaurant. Cross training is essential.

"We have taken a number of steps to blur the line between the front of the house and the back of the house. We consider our servers to be food professionals. They need to know as much about food and wine as a doctor does about medicine or a lawyer about the law. It gives them a deeper appreciation of how difficult it is for the kitchen to make that kind of food. And chefs who speak at tables can better empathize with what the front-of-the-house staff goes through."

Schmieding pointed out that servers at Trotter's don't simply recite a rehearsed spiel about the menu that evening. "They truly know food, which is important. For example, when a guest tells them that they

"I have come to appreciate the difficulty of doing what Trotter's does night after night, which is amazing because there is so much pressure now that Trotter's has attracted so much global press in the last few years. But the food and service are absolutely consistent. That's why Charlie has established himself as the greatest chef in the United States and certainly the equal of the world's great chefs like France's Alain Ducasse or Australia's Tetsuya Wakuda."

Ray Harris, Wall Street financier who has eaten at Charlie Trotter's nearly 300 times

have an allergy to onions, our server would know that the person would also likely be allergic to leeks or shallots. The untrained server would not recognize that."

At the end of their inspirational three-day visit, the Aramark managers returned home to Scotland to begin Trotterizing their own dining operations. One of the managers believes he now knows Trotter's recipe for success: "It's a combination of a good package that is consistently delivered because of constant reinforcement of the standards."

GIVING BACK

In the spirit of altruism, Trotter and the restaurant play an active role in the culinary community. At the James Beard House in New York City, he and his staff have put on cooking demonstrations to raise money for the organization. Trotter's was the first restaurant to host an out-of-house Beard event. Not long after the restaurant opened in 1987, Trotter invited ten top chefs from around the country to create a spectacular menu. All the proceeds of the event were donated to the Beard House, where he serves on the board of trustees. The restaurant hosted a Beard event for five years after that. Today, about twenty out-of-house Beard events are held every month throughout the country.

Charlie Trotter's took the lead role in the U.S. culinary community to honor the memory of the late chef Patrick Clark. Considered the best African-American chef in the country, Clark died of a rare blood disorder at the age of forty-two. He was the chef at the famed Tavern on the Green in New York City.

Trotter had always encouraged his good friend Clark to collect his own recipes and write a cookbook. Clark had begun the task, but it was unfinished at the time of his death, just a scrapbook of handwritten recipes. Trotter and his team, who know how to put together a cookbook, took it from there. They contacted leading chefs from around the country to contribute a favorite recipe as well as a favorite personal memory of the much-admired Clark.

The end result was a handsomely illustrated book titled *Cooking with Patrick Clark: A Tribute to the Man and His Cuisine*. Royalties from the $35 book were directed to a nonprofit fund to help support and educate Clark's five young children. To celebrate the book's publication, Trotter's hosted a special event at the restaurant in April 1999, which featured the late chef's cuisine. Similar events were held at restaurants throughout the country that month. "The whole culinary community, who are very generous people to begin with, rallied around one of their fallen colleagues," says Trotter.

TAKING THE SHOW ON THE ROAD

Trotter has given guest lectures at culinary schools, including the Culinary Institute of America, and cooking demonstrations at the American Culinary Federation. He estimates that he speaks or demonstrates for ten to twenty groups a year.

He is also active with the International Association of Culinary Professionals, the Illinois Restaurant Association, and the National Restaurant Association (NRA). He has hosted the IRA's annual event to award scholarships to budding chefs and restaurateurs. In Chicago, he serves as a member of the Culinary Advisory Board at the inner-city Kennedy-King College.

"It's imperative to help your own industry in a variety of different ways if you are successful at what you are doing. That's what we are trying to do here," he says.

SERVICE POINTS

To demonstrate a business's commitment to its community, consider these service points:

- Raise money, establish scholarships, or create a foundation to encourage young people to pursue careers in your field.

- Sponsor public service and works of charity; your employees will be proud to work for you.

- Host student field trips to your business. Employees get a charge out of working with young people.

- Mentor a young person by putting that person to work.

- Have employees speak to students about the passion they bring to their jobs.

- Offer to be a guest speaker at a school or university to share your knowledge and to inspire students to pursue excellence.

- Show respect for your business's neighborhood. Avoid garish signage and make sure your building reflects the neighborhood's character.

- Establish a relationship with your neighbors before opening for business.

- Provide a tour of your facilities to people in the neighborhood—from firefighters to schoolchildren.

- Generate additional streams of revenue by sharing your operational recipes with companies eager to emulate your standards and techniques.

- Contribute to the improvement of your industry's standards.

- Become active in industry associations and help the schools that will provide the future talent to help run your business.

CONCLUSION

It's the Journey, Not the Destination

I t would seem as if Charlie Trotter's has achieved its goal. It's the only restaurant in America to have won the Best Chef and Outstanding Restaurant awards from the James Beard Foundation in consecutive years. The *Wine Spectator* declared it the best restaurant in the world for food and wine. It has achieved financial and critical success. The accolades are endless, and the waiting list for a table on the weekend is nearly as long. Has Charlie Trotter's arrived?

"Well, we're not there yet," says Trotter. In fact, he's not quite sure where "there" is. "I'm more interested in the journey than the destination." Trotter says that he and his staff will continue "pushing it and pushing it, finding ways to get to the next level. We never get tired of what we do; we never get comfortable."

One of his favorite aphorisms is from race car champ/philosopher Mario Andretti, who once said: "If you're still in control, you're not driving fast enough." Trotter believes the restaurant can achieve even higher levels of service and culinary excellence. He will continue to drive himself and his staff to the outer limits of their abilities. And if they hit the wall, that's OK because that's the only way they'll find out if they're driving fast enough.

How has the restaurant gotten this far? Let's review some of the important aspects of Charlie Trotter's philosophy that enabled his restaurant to consistently deliver on its service promise:

- **PASSION.** Receptionist Makiko Hattori's job interview comment that she would execute a task with the same degree of enthusiasm regardless if she was doing it for McDonald's or the Ritz-Carlton still resonates with Trotter. He hires for passion, not necessarily for technical skill. He hires people who are just as enthusiastic about sweeping a floor as they are about presenting a menu. Each task demands the same level of passion. Small matters are no less significant than large ones; they all contribute to the big picture.

- **FLEXIBILITY.** Formal, robotically perfect service is not the goal. Although service needs to be technically proficient and highly disciplined, it also needs to be infused with a strong dose of humanity. Servers acquire a feel for each guest's needs and do whatever it takes to fulfill those requirements. They bend, they respond, they anticipate. Their sixth sense allows them to satisfy a need before the guest realizes he or she has one. Playing it by the book won't get the job done. Guests will never hear a service staff member utter the word "no."

- **EMPOWERMENT.** Trotter has a blind faith in his service staff's ability to do the right thing on behalf of a customer. They have complete authority to order an extra glass of wine or an extra course for a table to help push the guest's experience over the edge to fantastic. If something's not quite right, a server has the authority to deduct a charge from a check or even scrap the bill entirely. It would seem like a costly proposition, but the guest's satisfaction is worth the price. Empowering staff pays for itself many times over, says Trotter.

■ **FEEDBACK.** It's the lifeblood of the restaurant. Without knowing what customers truly want, Trotter's could never make the adjustments in its service and cuisine that make it so exceptional. Trotter's gathers feedback at several levels. The listening process begins when the guest first contacts the reservationist. Servers at the table also report customers' impressions to Trotter in the kitchen to help him and the chefs respond to each table's unique set of needs. Customer satisfaction surveys are carefully read, analyzed, and acted upon. Amends will always be made with a less-than-satisfied customer.

■ **QUALITY.** From the custom-made stoves and pristine foodstuffs in the kitchen to the expensive stemware and flatware in the dining room, Trotter's invests in the best. The equipment is meticulously maintained and every inch of the restaurant—no part of which is off limits to guests—is spotless. This expense and care tell the staff that they are working with the best, including the best customers and the best service staff in the business. Trotter reminds his staff, however, that each day they have to earn the right to work with the best by treating guests, colleagues, and the restaurant with the highest level of respect.

■ **PROFESSIONALISM.** Trotter treats his staff like the pros they are. Rather than hustle for tips, they're paid a guaranteed wage, and a handsome one at that. They also receive a benefits package. Servers wear business suits rather than uniforms, and Trotter meets with them each evening that he's in the restaurant as they prepare for what lies ahead that night and to reflect on the night before. There are opportunities for promotion to new positions or a managerial level.

■ **KNOWLEDGE.** Trotter's team on the floor know their stuff. They're as conversant about the food as most chefs are at other restaurants. They feel comfortable talking to chefs about a table's needs, even at the kitchen's most frenetic moments. During training, the service staff are exposed to the best wines and food-stuffs in the world. Trotter enhances their education by taking them to special events all over the United States and Canada.

- **TRAINING.** Forget the manual. Trotter's doesn't use a manual that accentuates following standard guidelines. Trotter's is all about possibilities. Service team members learn by observing and role playing. More veteran staffers critique new hires during role-playing sessions. No holds are barred. Staffers are carefully mentored over the course of their first year on the job. There is a continuous stream of advice and feedback.

- **MOTIVATION.** Trotter doesn't like the word—he prefers inspiration—but it's what he develops. He lights a fire under his staff with a variety of methods. He shows them classic, award-winning films to encourage their appreciation of fine craftsmanship. He might surprise an employee with a bonus in his or her check. He might invite an employee to a special event. He's also quick to reprimand an employee whose efforts are falling short of his standards. He believes a little anxiety is a valuable motivational tool.

- **COMMUNICATION.** The front-of-the-house staff's ballet-like precision on the floor boils down to their uncanny knack for communicating with each other. They listen to the guests and share intelligence about a guest's needs with each other. They express a great deal to each other with nonverbal communication. Their electronic communication system, invisible to the guests, also plays a role. Missteps are corrected, and management reinforces the right steps.

- **CHALLENGES.** Trotter doesn't let his staff get bored. He's constantly looking for ways to challenge them by assigning them new tasks. A server may become a sommelier or the general manager of the restaurant's retail outlet. A dining room manager may be tapped to coordinate the logistics of a program that brings more than a thousand students to the restaurant each year as part of a culinary education program.

- **ESPIRIT DE CORPS.** The overused cry of the service worker— "That's not my department"—is never heard at Trotter's. The whole restaurant is an employee's department. Employees are cross trained so they can assist in any situation. Trotter wants a team of jacks-of-all-trades. The front-of-the-house staff and the back-of-the-house staff have a strong sense for each team's respective challenges. When both teams work in concert, an evening will be especially fine and the food will taste even better.

- **LOYALTY.** In an industry where tenures tend to be short, Trotter has managed to maintain a veteran staff; many of his front-of-the-house staff have been with the restaurant for more than five years. "Trotterites" are often in great demand in the restaurant industry because of the skills and the outlook they've acquired. Talented staff members are often welcomed back after seeing how things operate in less-demanding environments. Trotter says they return with a greater appreciation of how things are done at his restaurant.

- **LEADERSHIP.** It starts with Trotter, who is much admired by his troops. They are struck by his indefatigability and his dedication. He daily demonstrates that no task is beneath him—from taking out the trash to conducting a tour for a guest. He treats each task with the same degree of respect. He has imbued his staff with a sort of "How would Charlie do it?" mindset.

- **COMMUNITY.** An employee's day starts the moment he or she enters the neighborhood, before he or she walks into the restaurant. Employees treat the neighborhood around the restaurant with great respect. Staff will often pick up a piece of trash or sweep the city-owned walkways and alleys around the restaurant. Employees are reminded that the person they cut off while competing for a parking spot on the street may turn out to be their customer that night.

- **GENEROSITY.** Trotter and the restaurant have raised hundreds of thousands of dollars a year by sponsoring fund-raisers or donating their time for cooking demonstrations or putting on private dinners in the homes of people who have won the restaurant's services in a charity auction. Trotter is equally generous with the culinary community, contributing dinners or advice to people in the industry. He has strong relationships with his fellow chefs throughout the country and the world. Charlie Trotter's Culinary Education Foundation raises about $180,000 a year to help pay for the educations of budding culinarians. Trotter believes that once a business is successful, it's in a position to give something back to the community. Trotter employees say they like the feel of a business that so willingly pitches in for worthy causes.

- **EXCEPTIONAL.** Trotter's staff will stop at nothing to make a guest feel welcome. Their efforts often go beyond the dining room. On nights when transportation is scarce, servers have given guests rides home—even in the middle of a blizzard. They have brought coats or jackets left behind to guests' homes or hotels. They've sent people home with goodies in a gift bag, and they've helped people calling the restaurant seeking advice on how to re-create a dish—even if it was one prepared at another restaurant. Trotter reminds his staff that if it weren't for the guests, "We'd never be able to pursue this unique philosophy and express ourselves in this unique way."

These lessons in service will guide Charlie Trotter's as it continues its remarkable journey.

INDEX

A

Allergies, 124, 150
American Culinary Federation, 218
American Society, 207
Andretti, Mario, 221
Anticipation, 32, 88, 136
Anxiety, importance of, 95, 224
Apocalypse Now, 65
Apologies, 144–45
Aramark, 214–17
Awards, 3, 14, 65, 221

B

Boeing Corporation, 108

C

California Culinary Academy, 18
Carle, Judi, 71, 99
Challenges, importance of,
    94–95, 98, 224–25
Chang, Belinda, 31, 36–37,
    54–56, 79–80, 84, 91, 93,
    107, 111, 126–27, 156,
    175–82, 187, 213–14
Change, 43–44, 94
Charities and fund-raisers, 186,
    206–7. *See also* Charlie
    Trotter's Culinary Educa-
    tion Foundation;

Community;
    Guest-Chef-for-a-Day
Charlie Trotter's
    awards won by, 3, 14, 65, 221
    celebrities at, 51
    criticism of, 64–65
    daily number of guests at, 19
    dining room dynamics in,
        129–38
    example evening at, 1–7
    exceeding customers' expecta-
        tions, 163–83
    importance of service at,
        13–14, 27–30, 34, 150
    investments in quality at, 3,
        20–22
    kitchen at, 6, 88
    menus at, 3–4
    out-of-house events, 185–91
    physical layout of, 67
    reasons for success of, 222–26
    reservations at, 2, 133–34, 139
    signage for, 209–10
    staff of, 21–23, 51–58,
        69–76, 122
    tours of, 6–7
    valet service at, 2, 30
    wine at, 4, 6, 28, 36–37,
        55–56, 89, 175–82

Charlie Trotter's Culinary Education Foundation, 37, 90, 201–6, 226
Chefs
in the dining room, 95, 125–26, 216
Guest-Chef-for-a-Day, 90, 206
visiting, 206, 217
Chicago magazine, 64, 65, 136
Clark, Patrick, 217–18
Close, Father James, 207–8
Communication
among employees, 121–22, 127–29, 138–40, 224
with customers, 113
Community. *See also* Charities and fund-raisers
culinary, 214–18
demonstrating commitment to, 219
giving back to, 201, 203, 226
local neighborhood as, 208–11, 225–26
Complacency, guarding against, 68–69
Complaints, 151–57. *See also* Feedback; Problems and mistakes
Conversations, interrupting, 30–31
Cookbooks, 99, 169, 189, 190, 217–18
Cooking demonstrations, 63, 188, 189–90, 217, 218

Cooking with Patrick Clark, 218
Coppola, Francis Ford, 65
Crain's Chicago Business, 64–65
Crawford, Janie, 114
Crissier, Switzerland, 19
Cronin, Kevin, 21, 66–67, 71, 88
Cross training, 37, 86, 95–100, 216, 225
Culinary Institute of America, 218
Customer satisfaction surveys, 151–58, 223
Customers/guests
as active participants, 135
building stronger bonds with, 119
chance encounters with, 212–14
customizing service for, 109
demanding or obnoxious, 20, 34–35, 80, 147–48
dining room dynamics, 129–38
exceeding expectations of, 163–83, 226
feedback from, 223
firing, 135
first-time, 109–10, 112, 116
misreading, 136–37
questions from, 113–15
reading minds of, 32, 138–39
relaxing, 115–16
returning, 107–11

D

Delays, 33, 146, 147

Departments, cooperation
among, 121–22, 141

Detail, attention to, 13–16,
23–25, 190

Dining room dynamics, 129–38

Dostoevski, Feodor, 63, 206

E

Employees. *See also* Chefs; Hiring;
Servers; Training

challenging, 37, 94–95, 98,
224–25

communication among,
121–22, 127–29, 138–40,
224

compensation plan for, 69–76

empowering, 61, 76–80, 222

espirit de corps, 67, 225

evaluations of, 72–73

firing, 50–51

knowledgeability of, 54–55,
66–67, 88–89, 216–17,
223–24

loyalty of, 225

motivating/inspiring, 61, 64,
65–67, 224

professionalism of, 223

providing leadership for,
61–64, 205–6, 225

rehiring former, 57–58

reprimanding, 35–36, 64

turnover of, 70

Empowerment, 61, 76–80, 222

Espirit de corps, 67, 225

Estrada, Francisco, 144–45, 166

Events, out-of-house, 185–91

Expediter position, 123–25

F

Feedback, 151–58, 223

Firing
customers/guests, 135
employees, 50–51

Fitzcarraldo, 65–66

Fitzgerald, Dan, 23–24, 57–58,
66, 68, 93, 127, 153, 165

Flexibility, importance of, 76–77,
79–80, 222

Floater position, 148–49

Food allergies, 124, 150

G

Gaya, Angelo, 207

Gayer, Michele, 194

Generosity. *See* Charities and
fund-raisers; Community

Giles, Christian, 30, 90–91, 109,
149, 153, 166, 174

Girardet, 19

Girardet, Fredy, 19

Godinez, Marvin, 21, 58, 127,
145, 150

The Goodman Theater, 207

Greater Little Rock Baptist
Church, 210

Guest-Chef-for-a-Day, 90, 206

Guests. *See* Customers/guests

H

Harvest of Hope, 92
Hattori, Makiko, 30, 35–36, 46–47, 51–52, 168–69, 222
Hegeman, Mary, 187
Herzog, Werner, 65
Hiring
  experience and, 43–44, 46
  interviews, 44–46, 49, 50
  nontraditional candidates, 43–44, 47–48
  for passion, 44, 46, 222
  re-, 57–58
  red flags, 45, 49
  tryouts, 50
Hotel Meridien, 18
Humor, 31, 146

I

Illinois Restaurant Association, 218
International Association of Culinary Professionals, 218

J

James Beard Foundation awards, 3, 14, 65, 221
James Beard House, 185–86, 217
Joffrey Ballet, 92
Johnson, Magic, 97, 127
Jordan, Michael, 63, 174

K

Kastrati, Ari, 84
Kennedy-King College, 218
The Kitchen Sessions with Charlie Trotter, 6, 169–70

L

Larson, Paul, 84–85, 87, 88, 90, 110, 130, 168, 186, 212
Leadership, 61–64, 205, 225
Lindgren, Aaron, 208
Literacy Chicago, 187, 207
Loyalty
  of customers, 105
  of staff, 225
Lyric Opera, 207

M

Make-a-Wish Foundation, 207
Meetings, 89–94, 154, 156
Mercy Home for Boys and Girls, 92, 207
Merges, Matt, 90, 92, 93, 96, 125, 126, 153, 204
Mistakes. *See* Problems and mistakes
Motivation, 61, 64, 65–67. *See also* Leadership
Moulin de Mougins, 207
Movies, 65–66

N

Napa Valley, 18
National Restaurant Association, 218

Neighborhood, respect for, 208–11, 225–26
New York, 18, 56, 186, 217

O
Off-site venues, 185–98

P
Paris, 18
Passion, importance of, 44, 64, 222
Performance evaluations, 72–73
Platt, Jason, 19, 37, 78, 84, 91, 145, 169
Preservice meetings, 89–94, 154, 156
Problems and mistakes, 32–33, 37–38, 85, 122–23, 143–51. *See also* Complaints; Feedback
Professionalism, 54, 223
Providence–St. Mel, 207

Q
Quality, investments in, 20–22, 223

R
Ravinia Music Festival, 207
Rehiring, 57–58
Relais & Chateaux, 2
Reprimands, 35–36, 64
Reservations, 2, 133–34, 139
Role-playing, 83–85, 224

Roman, Rene, 67–68, 84, 152, 169–70

S
Sam's Wine & Liquors, 213
Sandoval, Erwin, 123–25, 127, 164, 187–88
San Francisco, 18
Schmieding, Mitchell, 48–50, 56–57, 86–87, 88, 98, 105–6, 116, 127, 137, 148–49, 153, 170, 215, 216
Seating. *See* Dining room dynamics
Servers. *See also* Employees
  characteristics of good, 27–29, 33–34, 52–53, 137
  compensation plan for, 69–76
  empowering, 76–80
  knowledgeability of, 54–55, 66–67, 88–89, 216–17
  personality types of, 117–18
  personal touches of, 30–32, 137
  as professionals, 54, 70, 114–15
  role of, 112
  shift length for, 73
  table ownership and, 105–7
Service
  avoiding overly rehearsed, 138
  customizing, 109
  examples of poor, 15–16

Service, *continued*
    feedback and, 223
    flexibility and, 222
    nobility of, 13–14
    unwritten rules of, 138
Service points
    for attention to detail, 25
    for building customer relationships, 119
    for creating a service system, 159
    for delivering an extraordinary experience, 39
    for demonstrating community commitment, 219
    for empowering and motivating staff, 81
    for exceeding expectations, 183
    for hiring, rehiring, and firing, 59
    for melding different departments, 141
    for off-site venues, 198
    for training, 101
Signorio, Mark, 27–29, 33–34, 88, 100, 115, 128, 129–30, 135, 145–46, 147, 151, 154, 196
Sincerity, importance of, 46, 49
Sinclair, Gordon, 17, 18
Sinclairs, 17
Sinclair's North American Grill, 18
Slater, Jerry, 36, 78, 83–84, 85

Smiling, importance of, 116
Smith, Jason, 36, 145, 177
Sorensen, Kurt, 31, 32–33, 34, 35, 47–48, 52, 53–54, 67, 79, 112, 130, 131, 194–95
Spellman, Joseph, 175
Spruce, 52
Staff. *See* Employees
Stone, Larry, 175
Synchronicity, 128–29

T
Tavern on the Green, 217
Tipping, 74–76
Torres, Debra, 30, 52–53, 68, 84, 85, 133
Training
    cross, 37, 86, 95–100, 216, 225
    without manuals, 86, 101
    observing the flow, 88
    through role-playing, 83–85, 224
    shadowing process, 86, 98
Trotter, Bob, 17, 56
Trotter, Charlie
    birth of, 16
    college years of, 16–17, 206
    early career of, 17–19
    opens own restaurant, 19
    awards given to, 3, 14, 65, 221
    culinary community and, 217–18

daily schedule of, 62–63
guest speaking, 208
interacting with students, 61,
    201–6
leadership of, 61–64, 225
perfectionism/excellentism of,
    16, 35–36, 63
at preservice meetings, 89–92,
    94, 156
on the road, 62–63, 66,
    185–91
Trotter, Dona-Lee, 90
Trotter, Dylan, 90
Trotter, Lynn, 90
Trotter's To Go, 31, 91, 100,
    191–97
Turow, Annette, 196

U
University of Wisconsin, 16–17,
    206

V
Van Aken, Norman, 17, 18
Verge, Roger, 207
Vinaffair: Art of the Earth, 207
Vodak, Joe, 209

W
Watkins, Reggie, 204–5
Werner, Eric, 193–94
Wine, 4, 6, 28, 36–37, 55–56,
    89, 175–82
Wine Spectator, 3, 65, 146, 175,
    221

Z
Zernich, Sari, 98–99, 138,
    188–91